Contents

About *Math Centers, Grades 2–3* 2

Making a File Folder Center 3

Center Checklist 4

What's Missing? (number order) 5

Pizza Party (fractional parts) 15

Money Match (value of coins and bills; calculating amounts) 25

The Answer Is… (computation) 39

Pattern Puzzles (number patterns) 51

Exactly the Same (congruent shapes) 61

Money Machines (function tables with money amounts) 75

Perimeter and Area (calculating perimeter and area) 83

Measuring at the Circus (linear measure—U.S. customary, metric) 97

Time Flies (telling time; calculating elapsed time) 113

Read a Graph (reading bar, picture, and circle graphs) 128

Make a Graph (using data to create bar, picture, and circle graphs) .. 139

Name That Shape! (plane and solid geometric shapes) 151

Place Value Puzzles (place value—ones through millions) 169

Answer Key 187

About Math Centers
Grades 2–3

What's Great About This Book
Centers are a wonderful, fun way for students to practice important skills. The 14 centers in this book are self-contained and portable. Students may work at a desk, table, or even on the floor. Once you've made the centers, they're ready to use any time.

What's in This Book

Teacher direction page includes a description of the student task

Full-color materials needed for the center

Reproducible answer forms

How to Use the Centers
The centers are intended for skill practice, not to introduce skills. It is important to model the use of each center before students do the task independently.

Questions to Consider:
- Will students select a center, or will you assign the centers?
- Will there be a specific block of time for centers, or will the centers be used throughout the day?
- Where will you place the centers for easy access by students?
- What procedure will students use when they need help with the center tasks?
- Where will students store completed work?
- How will you track the tasks and centers completed by each student?

Making a File Folder Center

Materials

- folder with pockets
- envelopes or plastic self-locking bags
- marking pens and pencils
- two-sided tape

Steps to Follow

1. Laminate the cover. Tape it to the front of the folder.

2. Laminate the student direction page. Tape it to the back of the folder.

3. Place answer forms, writing paper, and any other supplies in the left-hand pocket.

4. Laminate the task cards. Place each set of cards in a labeled envelope or plastic self-locking bag. Place the envelopes and sorting mat (if required for the center) in the right-hand pocket.

Folder cover

Folder back cover
Student Direction page

Folder centers are easily stored in a box or file crate. Students take a folder to their desks to complete the task.

©2004 by Evan-Moor Corp. • Math Centers—Take It to Your Seat • EMC 3021

Center Checklist

Student Names

Centers

What's Missing?
Pizza Party
Money Match
The Answer Is…
Pattern Puzzles
Exactly the Same
Money Machines
Perimeter and Area
Measuring at the Circus
Time Flies
Read a Graph
Make a Graph
Name That Shape!
Place Value Puzzles

What's Missing?

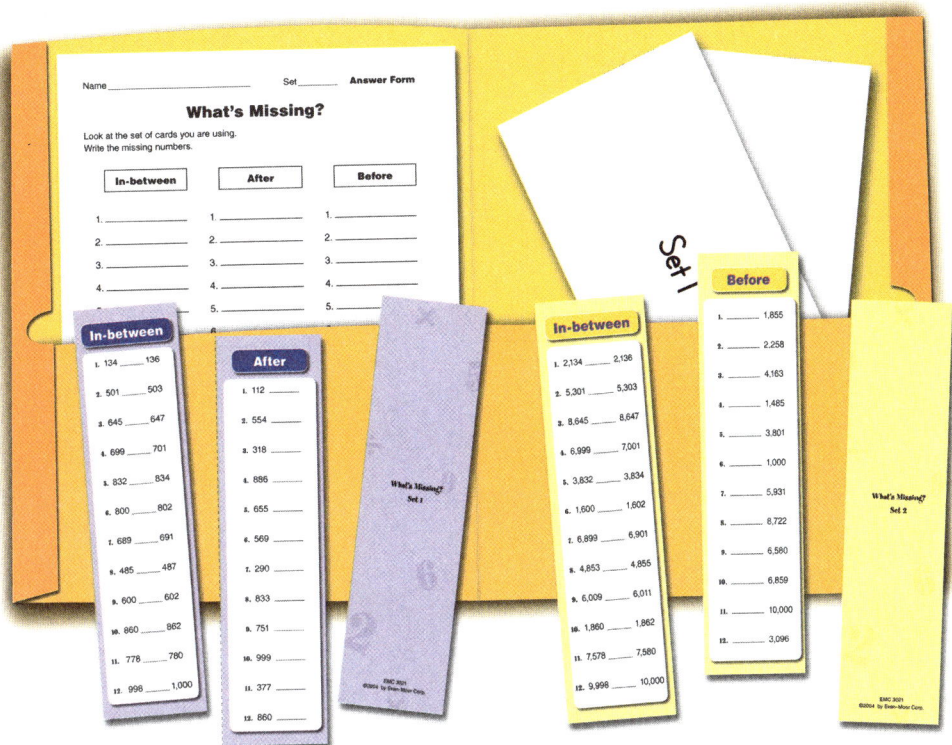

Preparing the Center

1. Prepare a folder following the directions on page 3.

    Cover—page 7
    Student Directions—page 9
    Task Cards—pages 11, 13

2. Reproduce a supply of the answer form on page 6. Place copies in the left-hand pocket of the folder.

Using the Center

1. The student selects a set of task cards and writes the set number on the answer form.

2. Next, the student selects the In-between card. He or she reads the card and writes the missing numbers on the answer form.

3. The student repeats the task using the After and Before cards.

©2004 by Evan-Moor Corp. • Math Centers—Take It to Your Seat • EMC 3021

Name _____ Set _____ **Answer Form**

What's Missing?

Look at the set of cards you are using.
Write the missing numbers.

In-between	**After**	**Before**
1. _____	1. _____	1. _____
2. _____	2. _____	2. _____
3. _____	3. _____	3. _____
4. _____	4. _____	4. _____
5. _____	5. _____	5. _____
6. _____	6. _____	6. _____
7. _____	7. _____	7. _____
8. _____	8. _____	8. _____
9. _____	9. _____	9. _____
10. _____	10. _____	10. _____
11. _____	11. _____	11. _____
12. _____	12. _____	12. _____

Bonus: Choose one of these numbers. Write that number and the next 9 numbers that follow it on the back of this form.

896   503   1,852   4,000

What's Missing?

What's Missing?

Follow these steps:

1. Choose a set of task cards.

2. Take an answer form and write the set number.

3. Take the **In-between** card from the set.

4. Write the missing numbers on the answer form.

5. Repeat with the **After** card.

6. Repeat with the **Before** card.

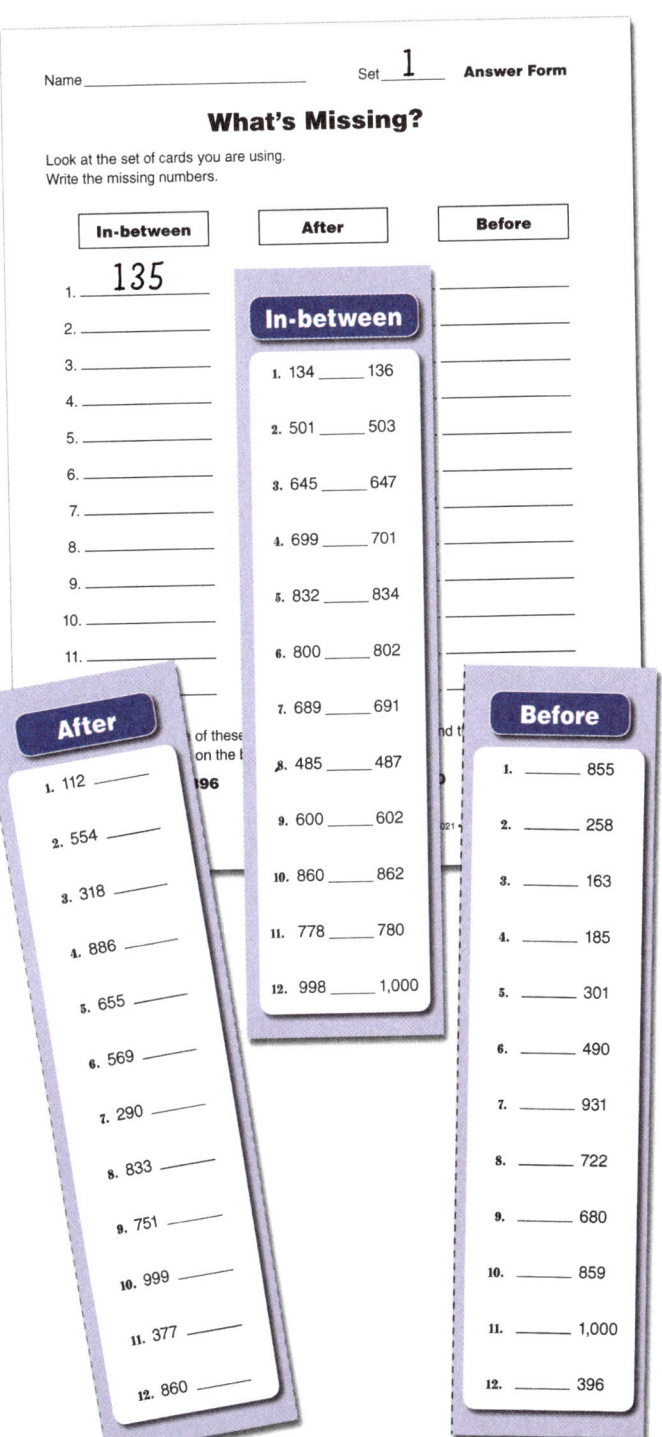

In-between

1. 134 _____ 136
2. 501 _____ 503
3. 645 _____ 647
4. 699 _____ 701
5. 832 _____ 834
6. 800 _____ 802
7. 689 _____ 691
8. 485 _____ 487
9. 600 _____ 602
10. 860 _____ 862
11. 778 _____ 780
12. 998 _____ 1,000

After

1. 112 _____
2. 554 _____
3. 318 _____
4. 886 _____
5. 655 _____
6. 569 _____
7. 290 _____
8. 833 _____
9. 751 _____
10. 999 _____
11. 377 _____
12. 860 _____

Before

1. _____ 855
2. _____ 258
3. _____ 163
4. _____ 185
5. _____ 301
6. _____ 490
7. _____ 931
8. _____ 722
9. _____ 680
10. _____ 859
11. _____ 1,000
12. _____ 396

©2004 by Evan-Moor Corp. • Math Centers—Take It to Your Seat • EMC 3021

What's Missing?
Set 1

What's Missing?
Set 1

What's Missing?
Set 1

EMC 3021
©2004 by Evan-Moor Corp.

EMC 3021
©2004 by Evan-Moor Corp.

EMC 3021
©2004 by Evan-Moor Corp.

In-between

1. 2,134 _____ 2,136
2. 5,301 _____ 5,303
3. 8,645 _____ 8,647
4. 6,999 _____ 7,001
5. 3,832 _____ 3,834
6. 1,600 _____ 1,602
7. 6,899 _____ 6,901
8. 4,853 _____ 4,855
9. 6,009 _____ 6,011
10. 1,860 _____ 1,862
11. 7,578 _____ 7,580
12. 9,998 _____ 10,000

After

1. 1,312 _____
2. 5,154 _____
3. 3,018 _____
4. 8,986 _____
5. 6,455 _____
6. 5,569 _____
7. 2,290 _____
8. 8,323 _____
9. 7,151 _____
10. 9,999 _____
11. 3,277 _____
12. 8,260 _____

Before

1. _____ 1,855
2. _____ 2,258
3. _____ 4,163
4. _____ 1,485
5. _____ 3,801
6. _____ 1,000
7. _____ 5,931
8. _____ 8,722
9. _____ 6,580
10. _____ 6,859
11. _____ 10,000
12. _____ 3,096

©2004 by Evan-Moor Corp. • Math Centers—Take It to Your Seat • EMC 3021

What's Missing?
Set 2

What's Missing?
Set 2

What's Missing?
Set 2

EMC 3021
©2004 by Evan-Moor Corp.

EMC 3021
©2004 by Evan-Moor Corp.

EMC 3021
©2004 by Evan-Moor Corp.

Pizza Party

Preparing the Center

1. Prepare a folder following the directions on page 3.

   Cover—page 17
   Student Directions—page 19
   Task Cards—pages 21, 23

2. Reproduce a supply of the answer form on page 16. Place copies in the left-hand pocket of the folder.

Using the Center

1. The student selects a set of task cards and writes the set number on the answer form.

2. The student selects two cards showing parts of a pizza and decides which of the pizza pieces represents the larger fraction.

3. Next, the student writes the fraction for each pizza part in the correct place on the answer form. For example: $\frac{1}{2} > \frac{1}{4}$

4. The student puts the cards back and repeats Steps 2 and 3.

©2004 by Evan-Moor Corp. • Math Centers—Take It to Your Seat • EMC 3021

Name _____

Set _____   **Answer Form**

Pizza Party

Pick two cards at a time. Write the fractions in the correct boxes.

Example:

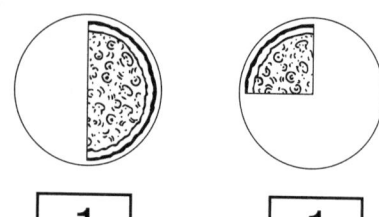

$\boxed{\frac{1}{2}}$ > $\boxed{\frac{1}{4}}$

1.
2.
3.
4. □ > □
5.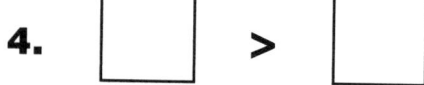
6.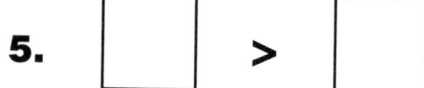
7.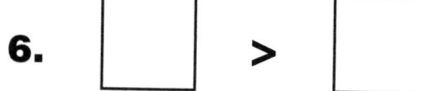
8. □ > □

Bonus: Take all nine cards and place them in order from the smallest to the largest. Write the fractions in order on the back of this form.

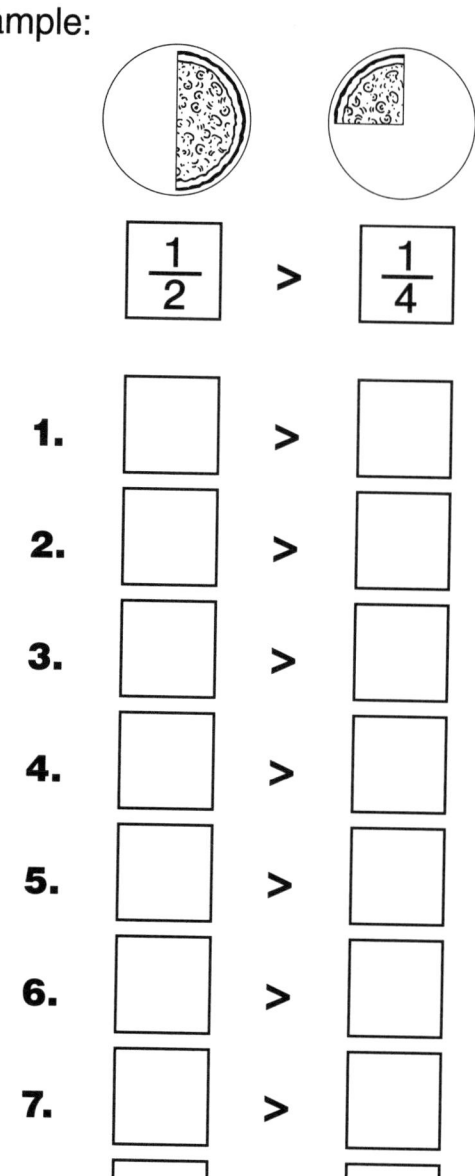

16 Math Centers—Take It to Your Seat • EMC 3021 • ©2004 by Evan-Moor Corp.

Pizza Party

Math Centers—Take It to Your Seat • EMC 3021 • ©2004 by Evan-Moor Corp.

Pizza Party

Follow these steps:

1. Choose a set of task cards.

2. Take an answer form and write the set number.

3. Take two cards. Look at the pizza part shown on each card.

4. Which piece is larger? Write the fractions in the correct place on the answer form.

$$\frac{1}{2} \quad > \quad \frac{1}{4}$$

5. Put the cards back and take two new cards. Repeat Step 4.

6. Do Step 3 and Step 4 six more times.

©2004 by Evan-Moor Corp. • Math Centers—Take It to Your Seat • EMC 3021

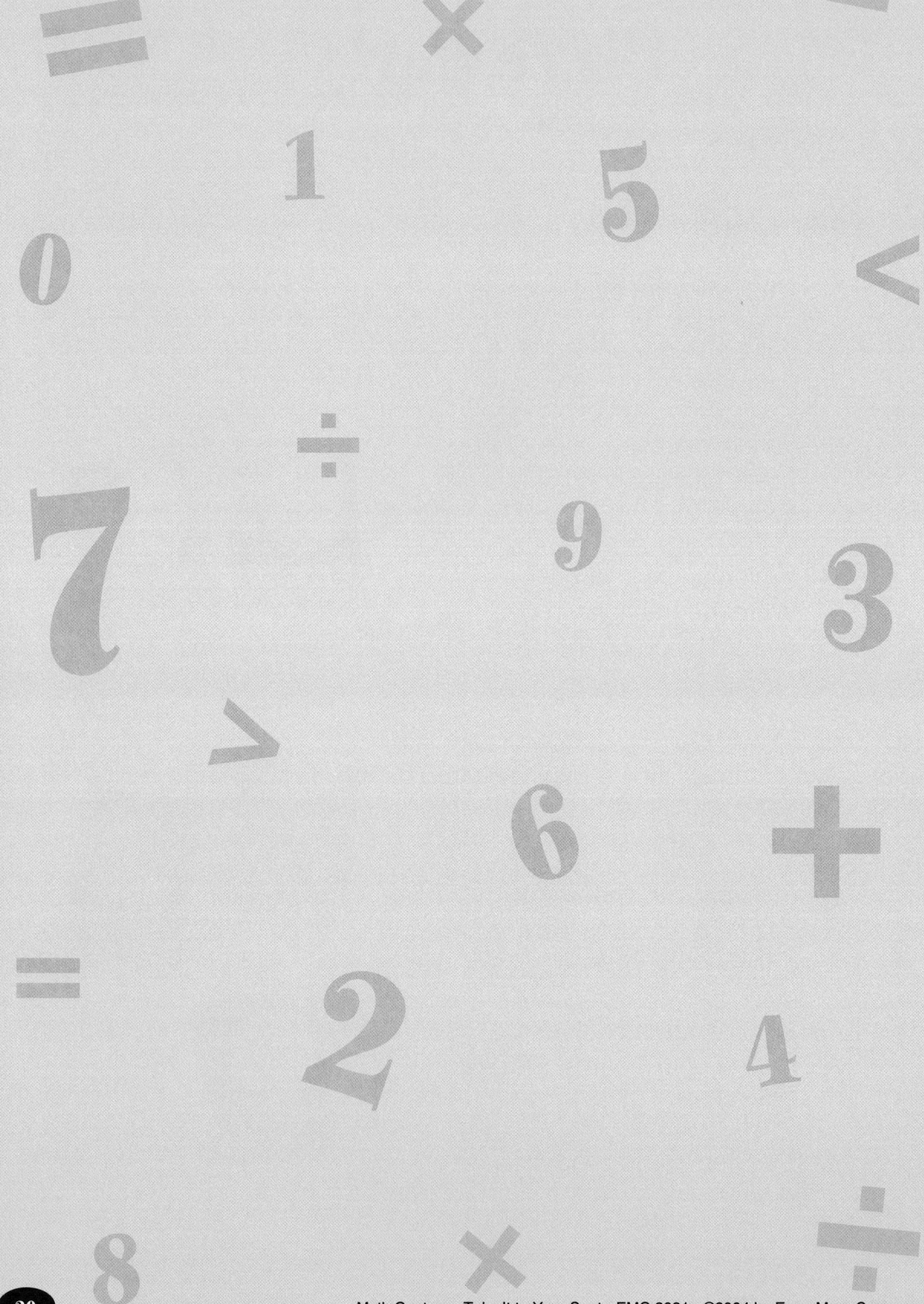

Pizza Party
Set 1

EMC 3021
©2004 by Evan-Moor Corp.

Pizza Party
Set 1

EMC 3021
©2004 by Evan-Moor Corp.

Pizza Party
Set 1

EMC 3021
©2004 by Evan-Moor Corp.

Pizza Party
Set 1

EMC 3021
©2004 by Evan-Moor Corp.

Pizza Party
Set 1

EMC 3021
©2004 by Evan-Moor Corp.

Pizza Party
Set 1

EMC 3021
©2004 by Evan-Moor Corp.

Pizza Party
Set 1

EMC 3021
©2004 by Evan-Moor Corp.

Pizza Party
Set 1

EMC 3021
©2004 by Evan-Moor Corp.

Pizza Party
Set 1

EMC 3021
©2004 by Evan-Moor Corp.

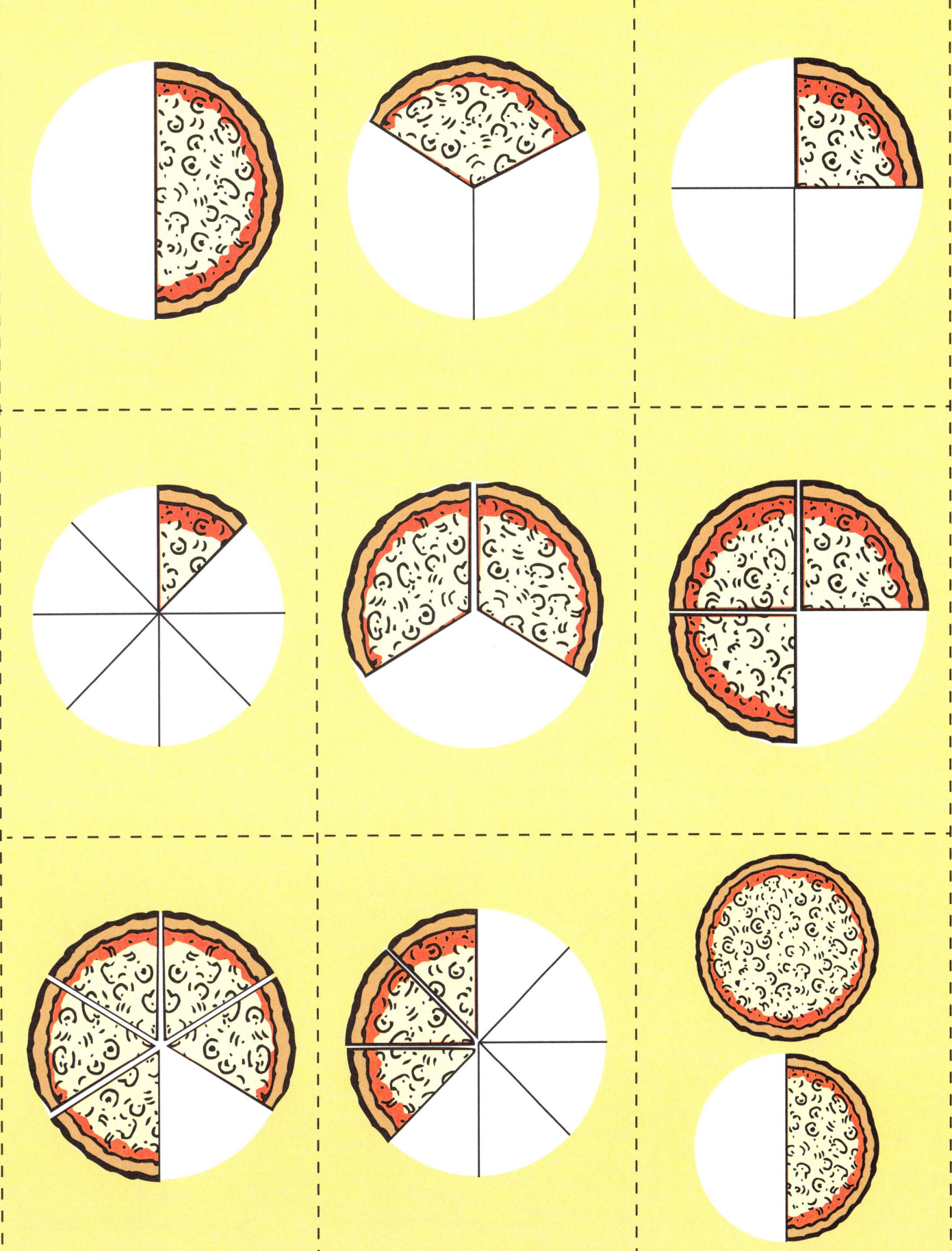

Pizza Party
Set 2

EMC 3021
©2004 by Evan-Moor Corp.

Pizza Party
Set 2

EMC 3021
©2004 by Evan-Moor Corp.

Pizza Party
Set 2

EMC 3021
©2004 by Evan-Moor Corp.

Pizza Party
Set 2

EMC 3021
©2004 by Evan-Moor Corp.

Pizza Party
Set 2

EMC 3021
©2004 by Evan-Moor Corp.

Pizza Party
Set 2

EMC 3021
©2004 by Evan-Moor Corp.

Pizza Party
Set 2

EMC 3021
©2004 by Evan-Moor Corp.

Pizza Party
Set 2

EMC 3021
©2004 by Evan-Moor Corp.

Pizza Party
Set 2

EMC 3021
©2004 by Evan-Moor Corp.

Money Match

Preparing the Center

1. Prepare a folder following the directions on page 3.

   Cover—page 27
   Student Directions—page 29
   Task Cards—pages 31–37

2. Reproduce a supply of the answer forms on page 26. Place copies in the left-hand pocket of the folder.

Using the Center

1. The student selects a set of task cards and the matching answer form for that set.

2. Next, the student matches the three cards that represent the same amount of money.

3. Then the student writes the sum amount on the first line and the numbers of the two matching money cards on the second line.

4. The student repeats the task with the remaining cards.

Name _____

Set 1   Answer Form

Money Match

Match three cards that show the same amount of money.

Sum	Cards
1. _____ ¢	____ , ____
2. _____ ¢	____ , ____
3. _____ ¢	____ , ____
4. _____ ¢	____ , ____
5. _____ ¢	____ , ____
6. _____ ¢	____ , ____

Bonus: Draw or write two ways to show $1.50.

Name _____

Set 2   Answer Form

Money Match

Match three cards that show the same amount of money.

Sum	Cards
1. $ _____	____ , ____
2. $ _____	____ , ____
3. $ _____	____ , ____
4. $ _____	____ , ____
5. $ _____	____ , ____
6. $ _____	____ , ____

Bonus: Draw or write two ways to show $1.50.

Money Match

28

Math Centers—Take It to Your Seat • EMC 3021 • ©2004 by Evan-Moor Corp.

Money Match

Follow these steps:

1. Take a set of task cards and the correct answer form.

2. Match 3 cards that show the same amount of money.

3. Write the money amount (sum) on the first line.

4. Write the numbers of the two cards that match the sum on the second line.

5. Repeat with the other cards.

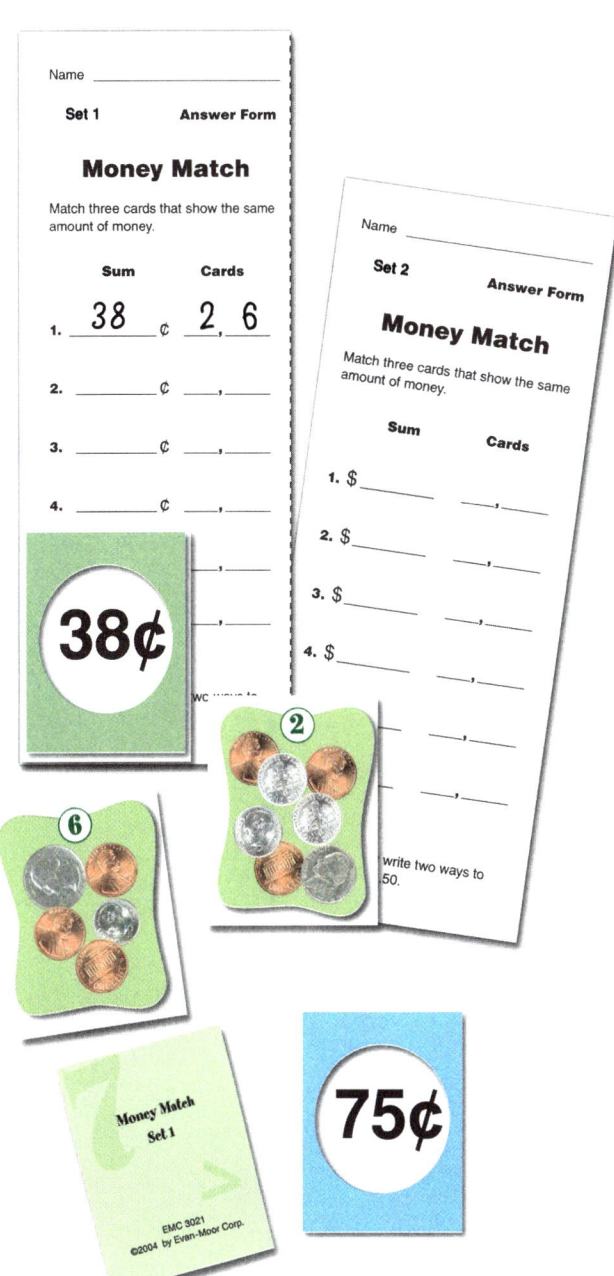

Money Match
Set 1

EMC 3021
©2004 by Evan-Moor Corp.

Money Match
Set 1

EMC 3021
©2004 by Evan-Moor Corp.

Money Match
Set 1

EMC 3021
©2004 by Evan-Moor Corp.

Money Match
Set 1

EMC 3021
©2004 by Evan-Moor Corp.

Money Match
Set 1

EMC 3021
©2004 by Evan-Moor Corp.

Money Match
Set 1

EMC 3021
©2004 by Evan-Moor Corp.

Money Match
Set 1

EMC 3021
©2004 by Evan-Moor Corp.

Money Match
Set 1

EMC 3021
©2004 by Evan-Moor Corp.

Money Match
Set 1

EMC 3021
©2004 by Evan-Moor Corp.

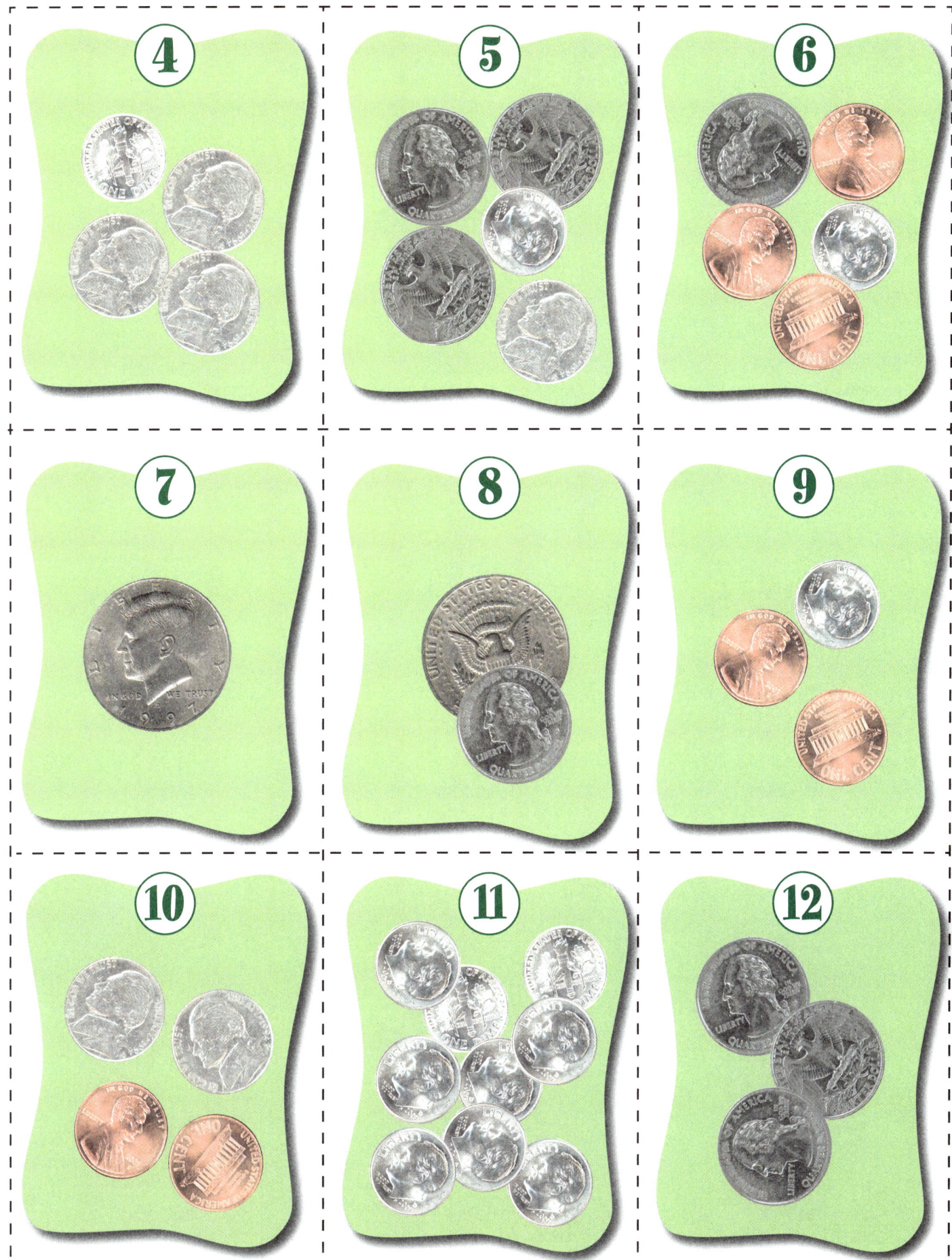

Money Match
Set 1

EMC 3021
©2004 by Evan-Moor Corp.

Money Match
Set 1

EMC 3021
©2004 by Evan-Moor Corp.

Money Match
Set 1

EMC 3021
©2004 by Evan-Moor Corp.

Money Match
Set 1

EMC 3021
©2004 by Evan-Moor Corp.

Money Match
Set 1

EMC 3021
©2004 by Evan-Moor Corp.

Money Match
Set 1

EMC 3021
©2004 by Evan-Moor Corp.

Money Match
Set 1

EMC 3021
©2004 by Evan-Moor Corp.

Money Match
Set 1

EMC 3021
©2004 by Evan-Moor Corp.

Money Match
Set 1

EMC 3021
©2004 by Evan-Moor Corp.

$0.80

$1.25

$1.93

$2.00

$2.55

$5.00

① ② ③

©2004 by Evan-Moor Corp. • Math Centers—Take It to Your Seat • EMC 3021

35

Money Match
Set 2

EMC 3021
©2004 by Evan-Moor Corp.

Money Match
Set 2

EMC 3021
©2004 by Evan-Moor Corp.

Money Match
Set 2

EMC 3021
©2004 by Evan-Moor Corp.

Money Match
Set 2

EMC 3021
©2004 by Evan-Moor Corp.

Money Match
Set 2

EMC 3021
©2004 by Evan-Moor Corp.

Money Match
Set 2

EMC 3021
©2004 by Evan-Moor Corp.

Money Match
Set 2

Money Match
Set 2

Money Match
Set 2

EMC 3021
©2004 by Evan-Moor Corp.

EMC 3021
©2004 by Evan-Moor Corp.

EMC 3021
©2004 by Evan-Moor Corp.

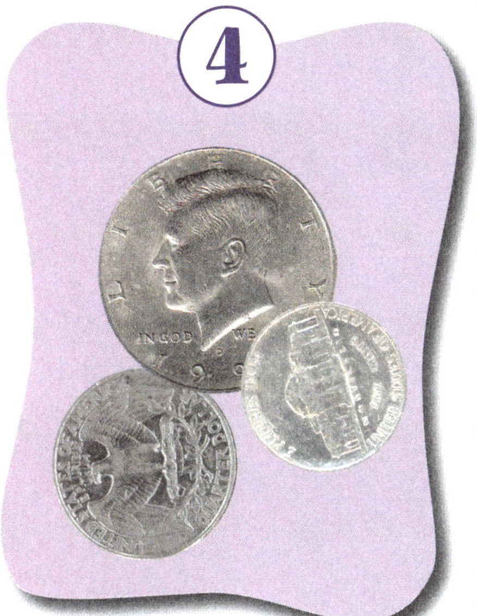
4

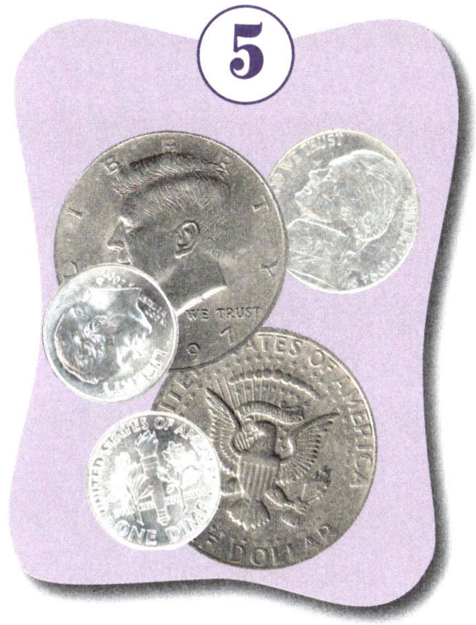
5

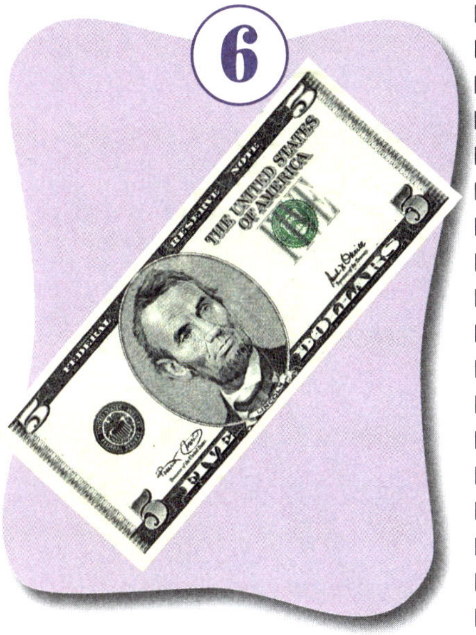
6

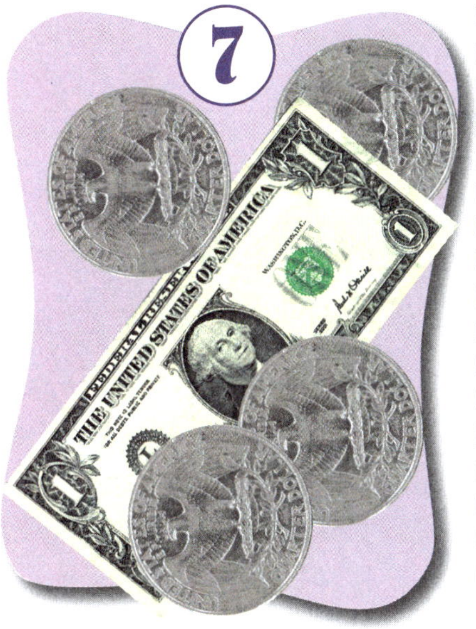
7

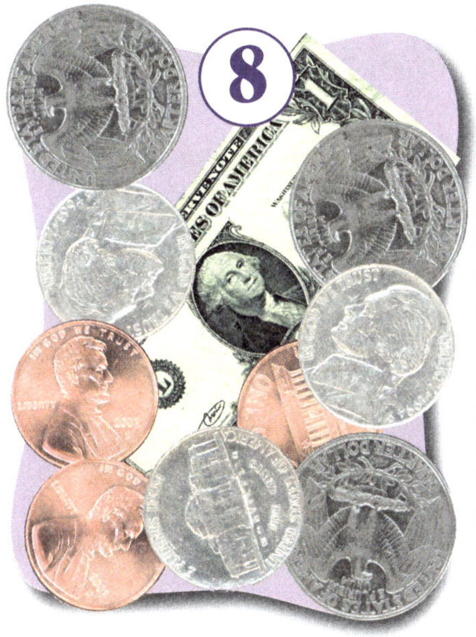
8

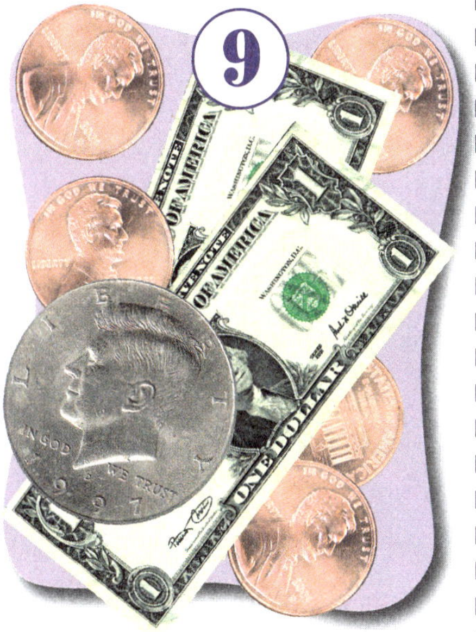
9

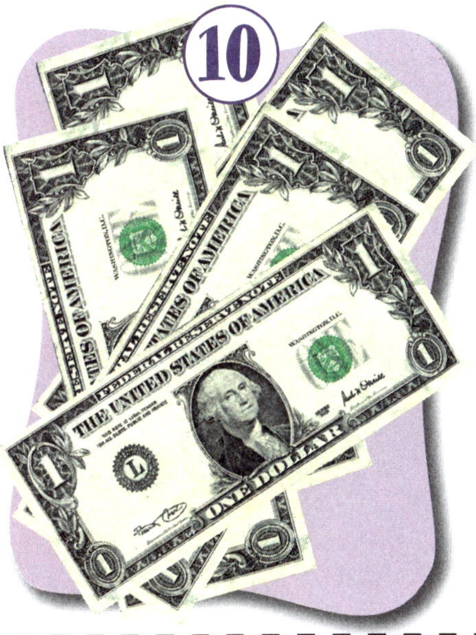
10

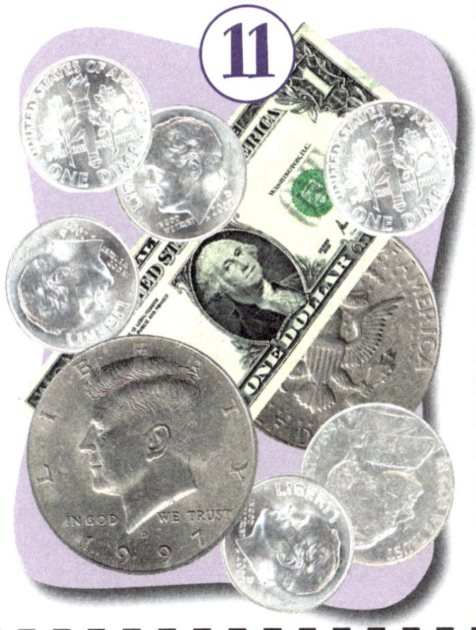
11

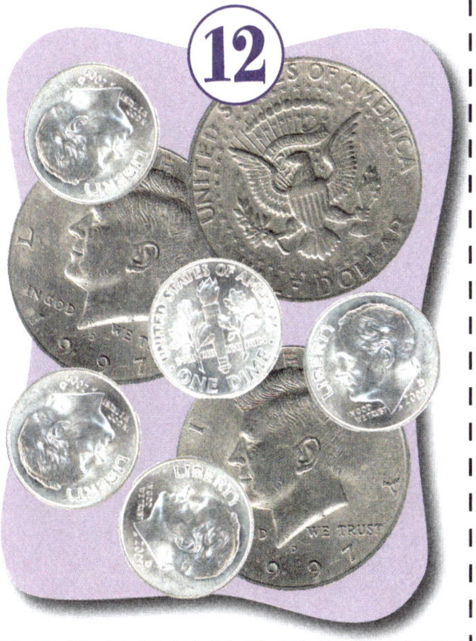
12

Money Match
Set 2

EMC 3021
©2004 by Evan-Moor Corp.

Money Match
Set 2

EMC 3021
©2004 by Evan-Moor Corp.

Money Match
Set 2

EMC 3021
©2004 by Evan-Moor Corp.

Money Match
Set 2

EMC 3021
©2004 by Evan-Moor Corp.

Money Match
Set 2

EMC 3021
©2004 by Evan-Moor Corp.

Money Match
Set 2

EMC 3021
©2004 by Evan-Moor Corp.

Money Match
Set 2

EMC 3021
©2004 by Evan-Moor Corp.

Money Match
Set 2

EMC 3021
©2004 by Evan-Moor Corp.

Money Match
Set 2

EMC 3021
©2004 by Evan-Moor Corp.

The Answer Is...

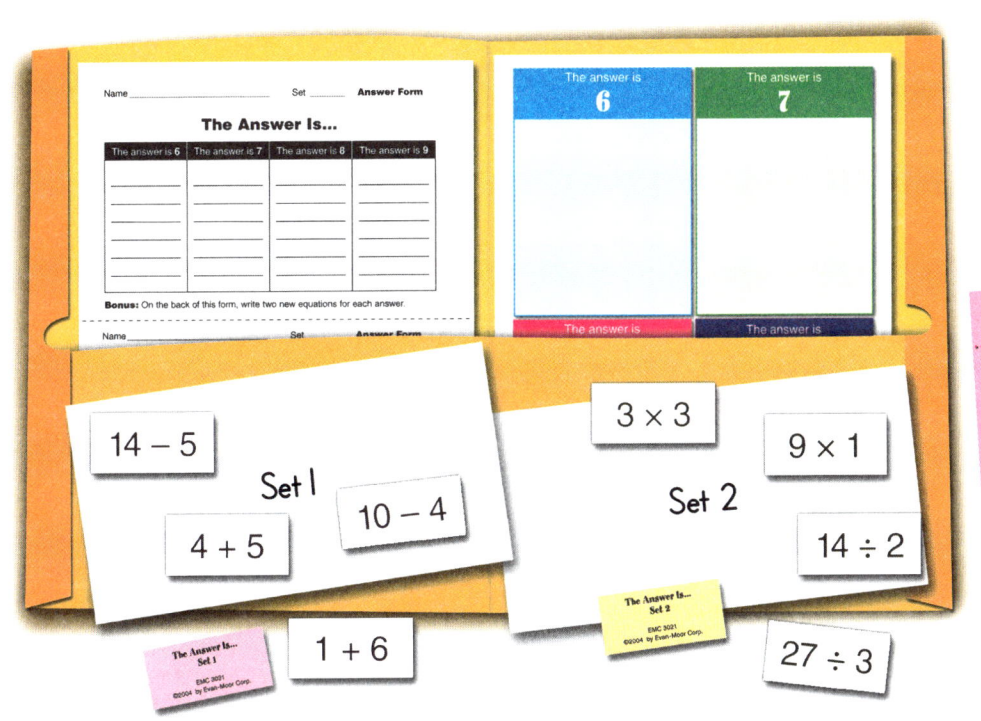

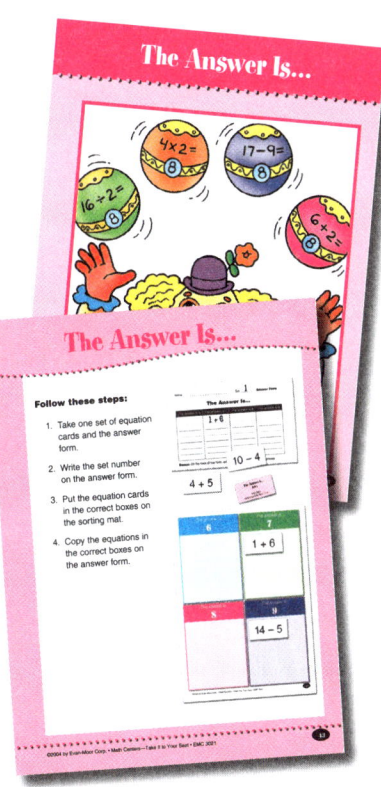

Preparing the Center

1. Prepare a folder following the directions on page 3.

    Cover—page 41
    Student Directions—page 43
    Sorting Mat—page 45
    Equation Cards—pages 47, 49

2. Reproduce a supply of the answer form on page 40. Place copies in the left-hand pocket of the folder.

Using the Center

1. The student selects one set of equation cards and writes the set number on the answer form.

2. The student places the equation cards in the correct boxes on the sorting mat.

3. Then the student copies the equations in the correct boxes on the answer form.

©2004 by Evan-Moor Corp. • Math Centers—Take It to Your Seat • EMC 3021

Name _____   Set _____   **Answer Form**

The Answer Is...

The answer is **6**	The answer is **7**	The answer is **8**	The answer is **9**
_____	_____	_____	_____
_____	_____	_____	_____
_____	_____	_____	_____
_____	_____	_____	_____
_____	_____	_____	_____
_____	_____	_____	_____

Bonus: On the back of this form, write two new equations for each answer.

- -

Name _____   Set _____   **Answer Form**

The Answer Is...

The answer is **6**	The answer is **7**	The answer is **8**	The answer is **9**
_____	_____	_____	_____
_____	_____	_____	_____
_____	_____	_____	_____
_____	_____	_____	_____
_____	_____	_____	_____
_____	_____	_____	_____

Bonus: On the back of this form, write two new equations for each answer.

The Answer Is...

42
Math Centers—Take It to Your Seat • EMC 3021 • ©2004 by Evan-Moor Corp.

The Answer Is...

Follow these steps:

1. Take one set of equation cards and the answer form.

2. Write the set number on the answer form.

3. Put the equation cards in the correct boxes on the sorting mat.

4. Copy the equations in the correct boxes on the answer form.

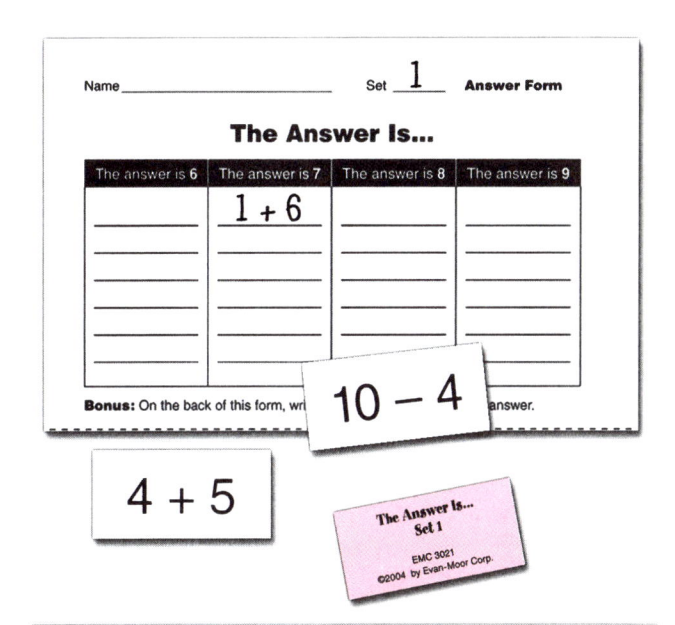

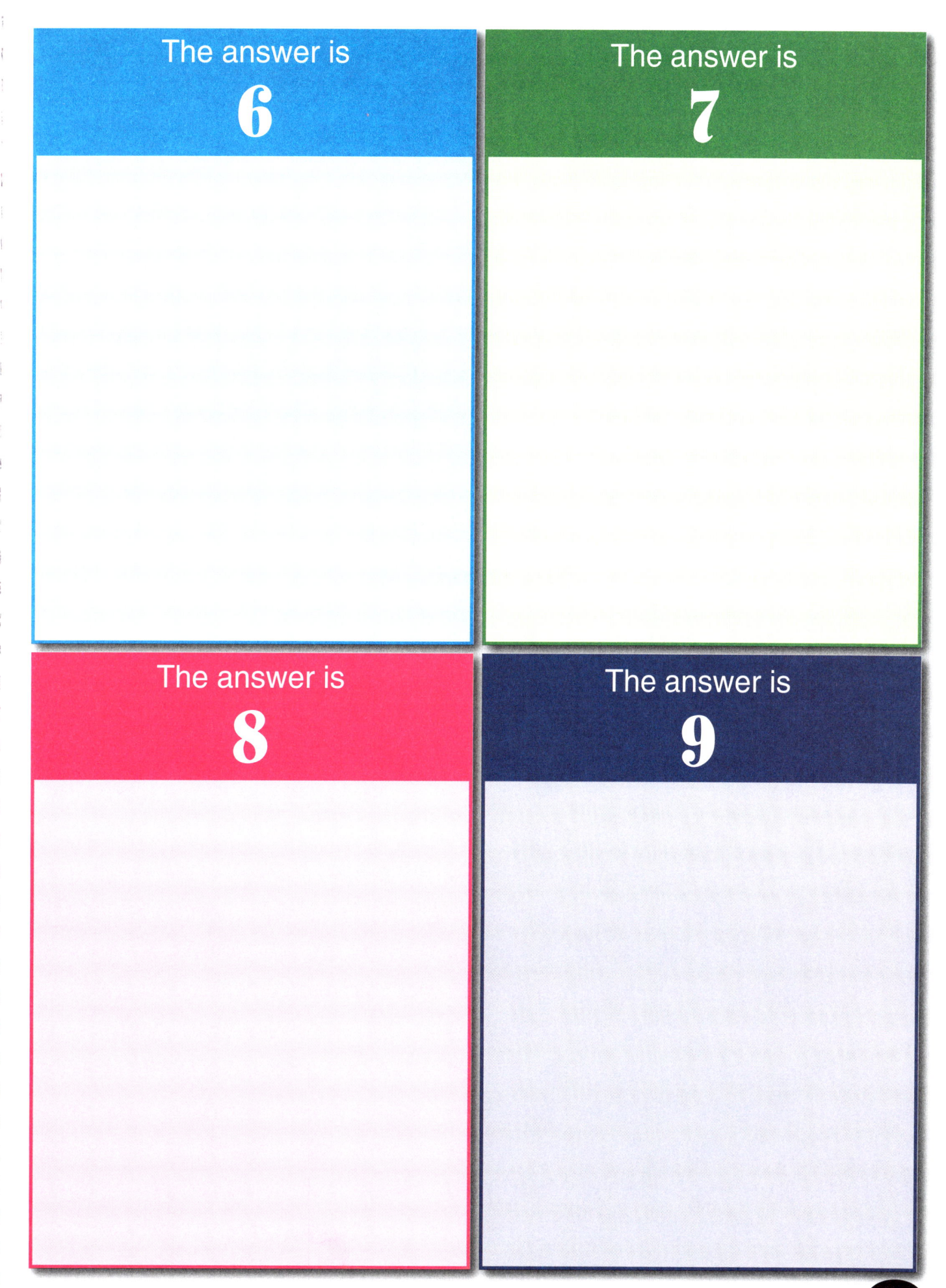

The answer is **6**	The answer is **7**
The answer is **8**	The answer is **9**

The Answer Is...

EMC 3021
©2004 by Evan-Moor Corp.

14 − 5	16 − 8	16 − 9
15 − 9	17 − 8	13 − 5
14 − 7	10 − 4	18 − 9
17 − 9	12 − 5	12 − 6
4 + 5	6 + 2	1 + 6
3 + 3	7 + 2	3 + 5
4 + 3	5 + 1	3 + 6
7 + 1	2 + 5	4 + 2

The Answer Is... Set 1	The Answer Is... Set 1	The Answer Is... Set 1
EMC 3021 ©2004 by Evan-Moor Corp.	EMC 3021 ©2004 by Evan-Moor Corp.	EMC 3021 ©2004 by Evan-Moor Corp.
The Answer Is... Set 1	The Answer Is... Set 1	The Answer Is... Set 1
EMC 3021 ©2004 by Evan-Moor Corp.	EMC 3021 ©2004 by Evan-Moor Corp.	EMC 3021 ©2004 by Evan-Moor Corp.
The Answer Is... Set 1	The Answer Is... Set 1	The Answer Is... Set 1
EMC 3021 ©2004 by Evan-Moor Corp.	EMC 3021 ©2004 by Evan-Moor Corp.	EMC 3021 ©2004 by Evan-Moor Corp.
The Answer Is... Set 1	The Answer Is... Set 1	The Answer Is... Set 1
EMC 3021 ©2004 by Evan-Moor Corp.	EMC 3021 ©2004 by Evan-Moor Corp.	EMC 3021 ©2004 by Evan-Moor Corp.
The Answer Is... Set 1	The Answer Is... Set 1	The Answer Is... Set 1
EMC 3021 ©2004 by Evan-Moor Corp.	EMC 3021 ©2004 by Evan-Moor Corp.	EMC 3021 ©2004 by Evan-Moor Corp.
The Answer Is... Set 1	The Answer Is... Set 1	The Answer Is... Set 1
EMC 3021 ©2004 by Evan-Moor Corp.	EMC 3021 ©2004 by Evan-Moor Corp.	EMC 3021 ©2004 by Evan-Moor Corp.
The Answer Is... Set 1	The Answer Is... Set 1	The Answer Is... Set 1
EMC 3021 ©2004 by Evan-Moor Corp.	EMC 3021 ©2004 by Evan-Moor Corp.	EMC 3021 ©2004 by Evan-Moor Corp.
The Answer Is... Set 1	The Answer Is... Set 1	The Answer Is... Set 1
EMC 3021 ©2004 by Evan-Moor Corp.	EMC 3021 ©2004 by Evan-Moor Corp.	EMC 3021 ©2004 by Evan-Moor Corp.

12 − 6	3 + 4	6 + 2
9 × 1	10 − 4	7 × 1
4 × 2	3 × 3	2 × 3
16 − 9	14 − 6	18 ÷ 2
12 ÷ 2	14 ÷ 2	2 × 4
17 − 8	16 ÷ 2	35 ÷ 5
32 ÷ 4	27 ÷ 3	18 ÷ 3
21 ÷ 3	6 + 3	30 ÷ 5

The Answer Is... **Set 2** EMC 3021 ©2004 by Evan-Moor Corp.	**The Answer Is...** **Set 2** EMC 3021 ©2004 by Evan-Moor Corp.	**The Answer Is...** **Set 2** EMC 3021 ©2004 by Evan-Moor Corp.
The Answer Is... **Set 2** EMC 3021 ©2004 by Evan-Moor Corp.	**The Answer Is...** **Set 2** EMC 3021 ©2004 by Evan-Moor Corp.	**The Answer Is...** **Set 2** EMC 3021 ©2004 by Evan-Moor Corp.
The Answer Is... **Set 2** EMC 3021 ©2004 by Evan-Moor Corp.	**The Answer Is...** **Set 2** EMC 3021 ©2004 by Evan-Moor Corp.	**The Answer Is...** **Set 2** EMC 3021 ©2004 by Evan-Moor Corp.
The Answer Is... **Set 2** EMC 3021 ©2004 by Evan-Moor Corp.	**The Answer Is...** **Set 2** EMC 3021 ©2004 by Evan-Moor Corp.	**The Answer Is...** **Set 2** EMC 3021 ©2004 by Evan-Moor Corp.
The Answer Is... **Set 2** EMC 3021 ©2004 by Evan-Moor Corp.	**The Answer Is...** **Set 2** EMC 3021 ©2004 by Evan-Moor Corp.	**The Answer Is...** **Set 2** EMC 3021 ©2004 by Evan-Moor Corp.
The Answer Is... **Set 2** EMC 3021 ©2004 by Evan-Moor Corp.	**The Answer Is...** **Set 2** EMC 3021 ©2004 by Evan-Moor Corp.	**The Answer Is...** **Set 2** EMC 3021 ©2004 by Evan-Moor Corp.
The Answer Is... **Set 2** EMC 3021 ©2004 by Evan-Moor Corp.	**The Answer Is...** **Set 2** EMC 3021 ©2004 by Evan-Moor Corp.	**The Answer Is...** **Set 2** EMC 3021 ©2004 by Evan-Moor Corp.
The Answer Is... **Set 2** EMC 3021 ©2004 by Evan-Moor Corp.	**The Answer Is...** **Set 2** EMC 3021 ©2004 by Evan-Moor Corp.	**The Answer Is...** **Set 2** EMC 3021 ©2004 by Evan-Moor Corp.

Pattern Puzzles

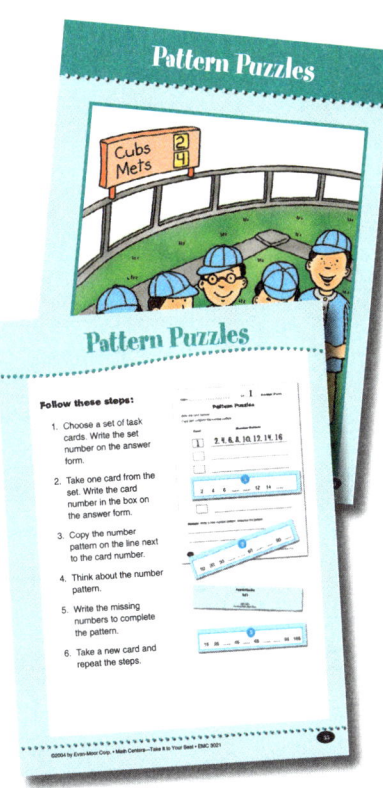

Preparing the Center

1. Prepare a folder following the directions on page 3.

    Cover—page 53
    Student Directions—page 55
    Task Cards—pages 57, 59

2. Reproduce a supply of the answer form on page 52. Place copies in the left-hand pocket of the folder.

Using the Center

1. The student selects a set of task cards and writes the set number on the answer form.

2. Next, the student takes one card from the set and writes its number in the box on the answer form.

3. Then the student copies the number pattern on the line and fills in the missing numbers to complete the pattern.

4. Finally, the student repeats Steps 2 and 3 with other cards in the set.

©2004 by Evan-Moor Corp. • Math Centers—Take It to Your Seat • EMC 3021

51

Name _____ Set _____ **Answer Form**

Pattern Puzzles

Write the card number.

Copy and complete the number pattern.

Card　　　　　　　　　**Number Pattern**

☐　　　_____

☐　　　_____

☐　　　_____

☐　　　_____

☐　　　_____

☐　　　_____

Bonus: Write a new number pattern. Describe the pattern.

_____

_____

Pattern Puzzles

Pattern Puzzles

Follow these steps:

1. Choose a set of task cards. Write the set number on the answer form.

2. Take one card from the set. Write the card number in the box on the answer form.

3. Copy the number pattern on the line next to the card number.

4. Think about the number pattern.

5. Write the missing numbers to complete the pattern.

6. Take a new card and repeat the steps.

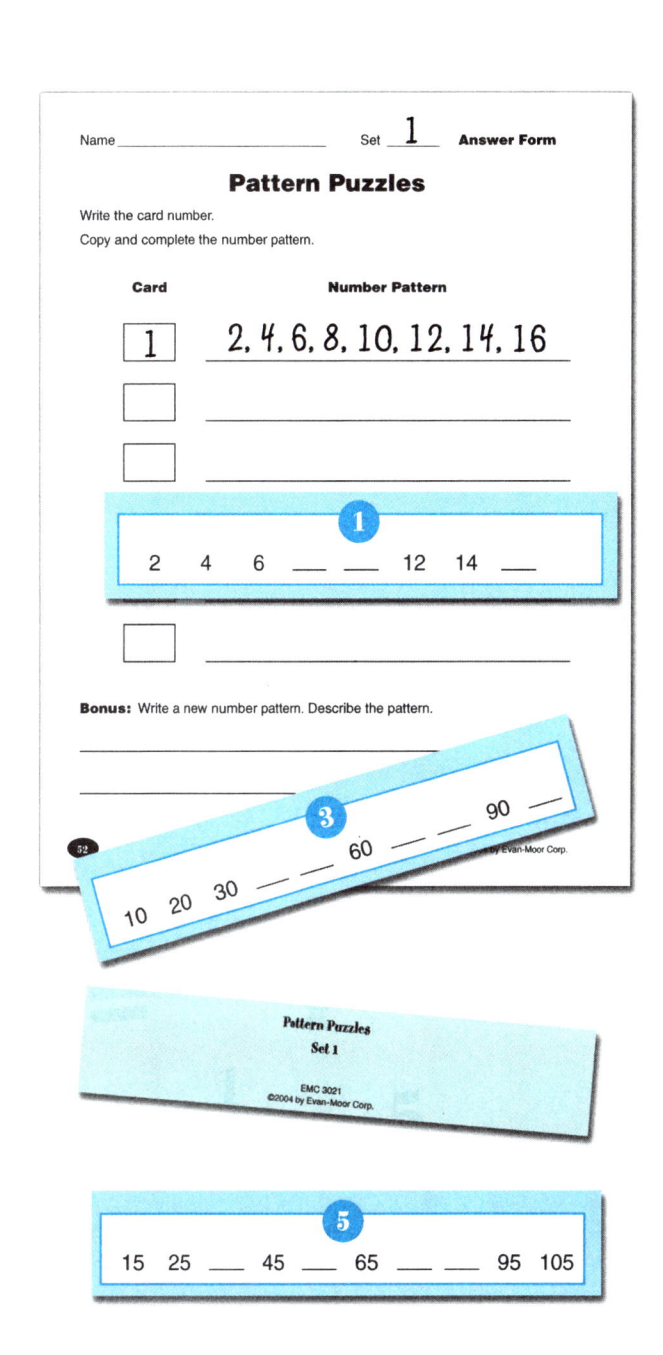

1

2   4   6   ___   ___   12   14   ___

2

5   10   ___   20   ___   ___   35   ___   45   ___

3

10   20   30   ___   ___   60   ___   ___   90   ___

4

3   6   9   ___   15   ___   ___   24   27   ___

5

15   25   ___   45   ___   65   ___   ___   95   105

6

2   22   3   33   ___   44   ___   ___   ___   ___

Pattern Puzzles
Set 1

EMC 3021
©2004 by Evan-Moor Corp.

Pattern Puzzles
Set 1

EMC 3021
©2004 by Evan-Moor Corp.

Pattern Puzzles
Set 1

EMC 3021
©2004 by Evan-Moor Corp.

Pattern Puzzles
Set 1

EMC 3021
©2004 by Evan-Moor Corp.

Pattern Puzzles
Set 1

EMC 3021
©2004 by Evan-Moor Corp.

Pattern Puzzles
Set 1

EMC 3021
©2004 by Evan-Moor Corp.

1
9   18   27   ___   ___   ___

2
3   8   7   12   ___   ___   ___

3
50   55   40   45   ___   ___   ___

4
100   150   200   ___   ___   ___   ___

5
1   3   2   4   3   ___   ___   ___

6
3   6   12   ___   ___   ___

Pattern Puzzles

Set 2

EMC 3021
©2004 by Evan-Moor Corp.

Pattern Puzzles

Set 2

EMC 3021
©2004 by Evan-Moor Corp.

Pattern Puzzles

Set 2

EMC 3021
©2004 by Evan-Moor Corp.

Pattern Puzzles

Set 2

EMC 3021
©2004 by Evan-Moor Corp.

Pattern Puzzles

Set 2

EMC 3021
©2004 by Evan-Moor Corp.

Pattern Puzzles

Set 2

EMC 3021
©2004 by Evan-Moor Corp.

Exactly the Same

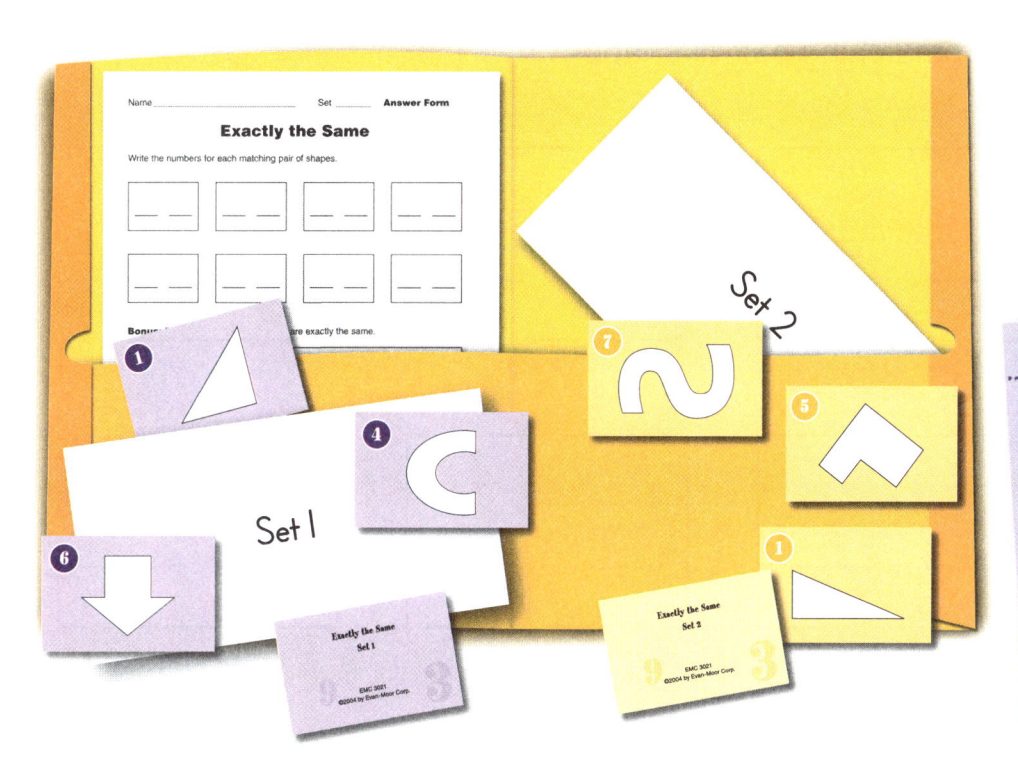

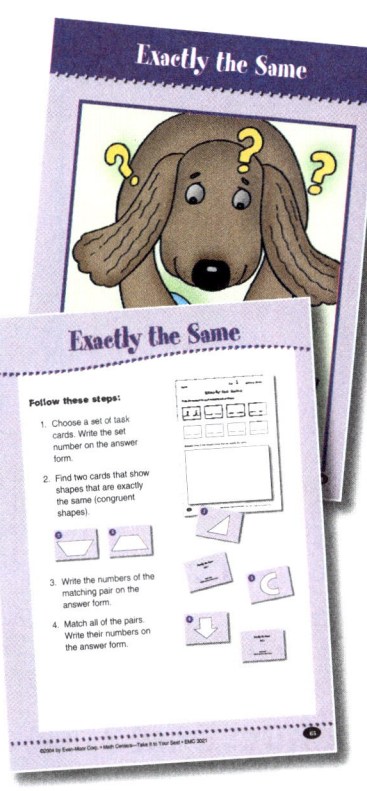

Preparing the Center

1. Prepare a folder following the directions on page 3.

   Cover—page 63
   Student Directions—page 65
   Task Cards—pages 67–73

2. Reproduce a supply of the answer form on page 62. Place copies in the left-hand pocket of the folder.

Using the Center

1. The student selects a set of task cards and writes the set number on the answer form.

2. Then the student finds two cards that show congruent shapes and writes the numbers of the matching pair on the answer form.

3. The student continues until all pairs have been matched.

Name _____ Set _____ **Answer Form**

Exactly the Same

Write the numbers for each matching pair of shapes.

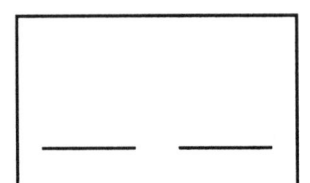

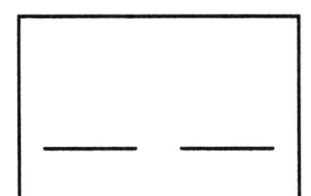

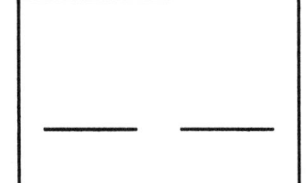

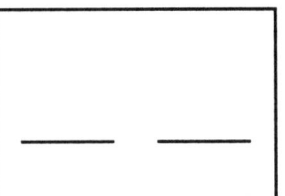

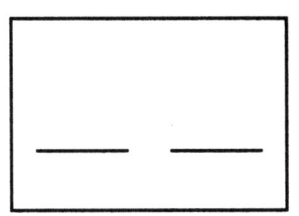

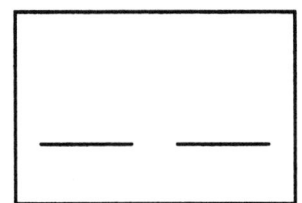

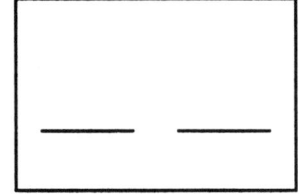

| ___ ___ | ___ ___ | ___ ___ | ___ ___ |

| ___ ___ | ___ ___ | ___ ___ | ___ ___ |

Bonus: Draw 2 new shapes below that are exactly the same.

62   Math Centers—Take It to Your Seat • EMC 3021 • ©2004 by Evan-Moor Corp.

Exactly the Same

Exactly the Same

Follow these steps:

1. Choose a set of task cards. Write the set number on the answer form.

2. Find two cards that show shapes that are exactly the same (congruent shapes).

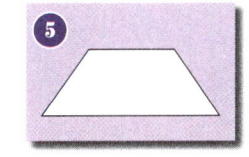

3. Write the numbers of the matching pair on the answer form.

4. Match all of the pairs. Write their numbers on the answer form.

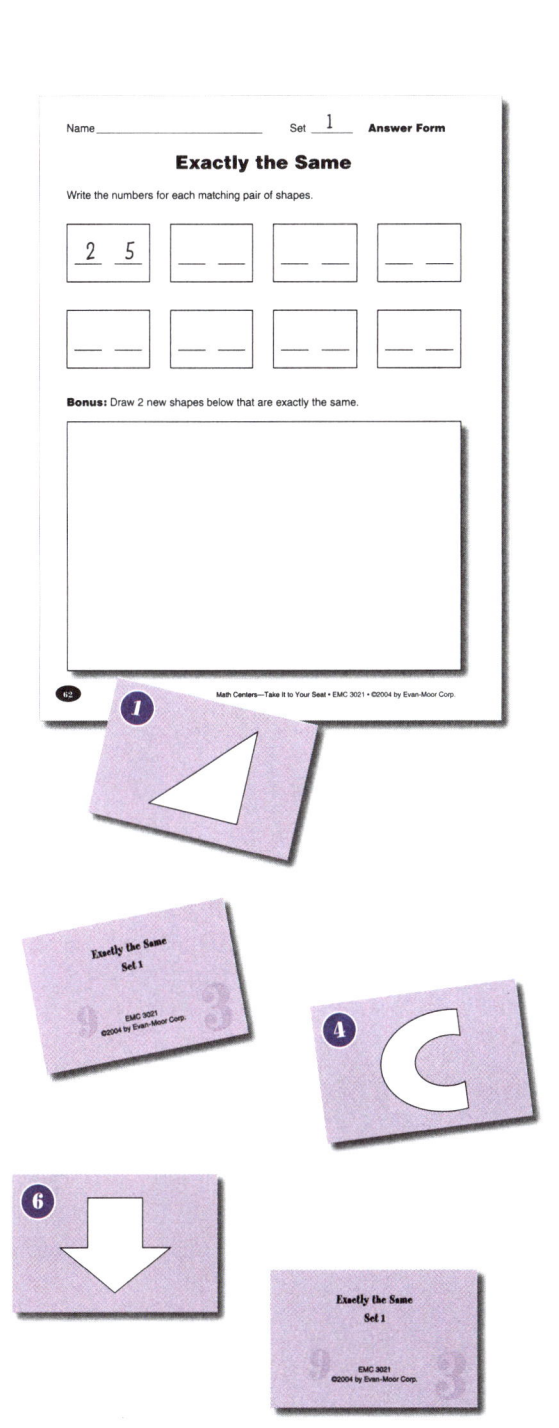

©2004 by Evan-Moor Corp. • Math Centers—Take It to Your Seat • EMC 3021

65

1
2
3
4
5
6
7
8

©2004 by Evan-Moor Corp. • Math Centers—Take It to Your Seat • EMC 3021

Exactly the Same
Set 1

EMC 3021
©2004 by Evan-Moor Corp.

Exactly the Same
Set 1

EMC 3021
©2004 by Evan-Moor Corp.

Exactly the Same
Set 1

EMC 3021
©2004 by Evan-Moor Corp.

Exactly the Same
Set 1

EMC 3021
©2004 by Evan-Moor Corp.

Exactly the Same
Set 1

EMC 3021
©2004 by Evan-Moor Corp.

Exactly the Same
Set 1

EMC 3021
©2004 by Evan-Moor Corp.

Exactly the Same
Set 1

EMC 3021
©2004 by Evan-Moor Corp.

Exactly the Same
Set 1

EMC 3021
©2004 by Evan-Moor Corp.

9
10
11
12
13
14
15
16

©2004 by Evan-Moor Corp. • Math Centers—Take It to Your Seat • EMC 3021

Exactly the Same
Set 1

EMC 3021
©2004 by Evan-Moor Corp.

Exactly the Same
Set 1

EMC 3021
©2004 by Evan-Moor Corp.

Exactly the Same
Set 1

EMC 3021
©2004 by Evan-Moor Corp.

Exactly the Same
Set 1

EMC 3021
©2004 by Evan-Moor Corp.

Exactly the Same
Set 1

EMC 3021
©2004 by Evan-Moor Corp.

Exactly the Same
Set 1

EMC 3021
©2004 by Evan-Moor Corp.

Exactly the Same
Set 1

EMC 3021
©2004 by Evan-Moor Corp.

Exactly the Same
Set 1

EMC 3021
©2004 by Evan-Moor Corp.

© 2004 by Evan-Moor Corp. • Math Centers—Take It to Your Seat • EMC 3021

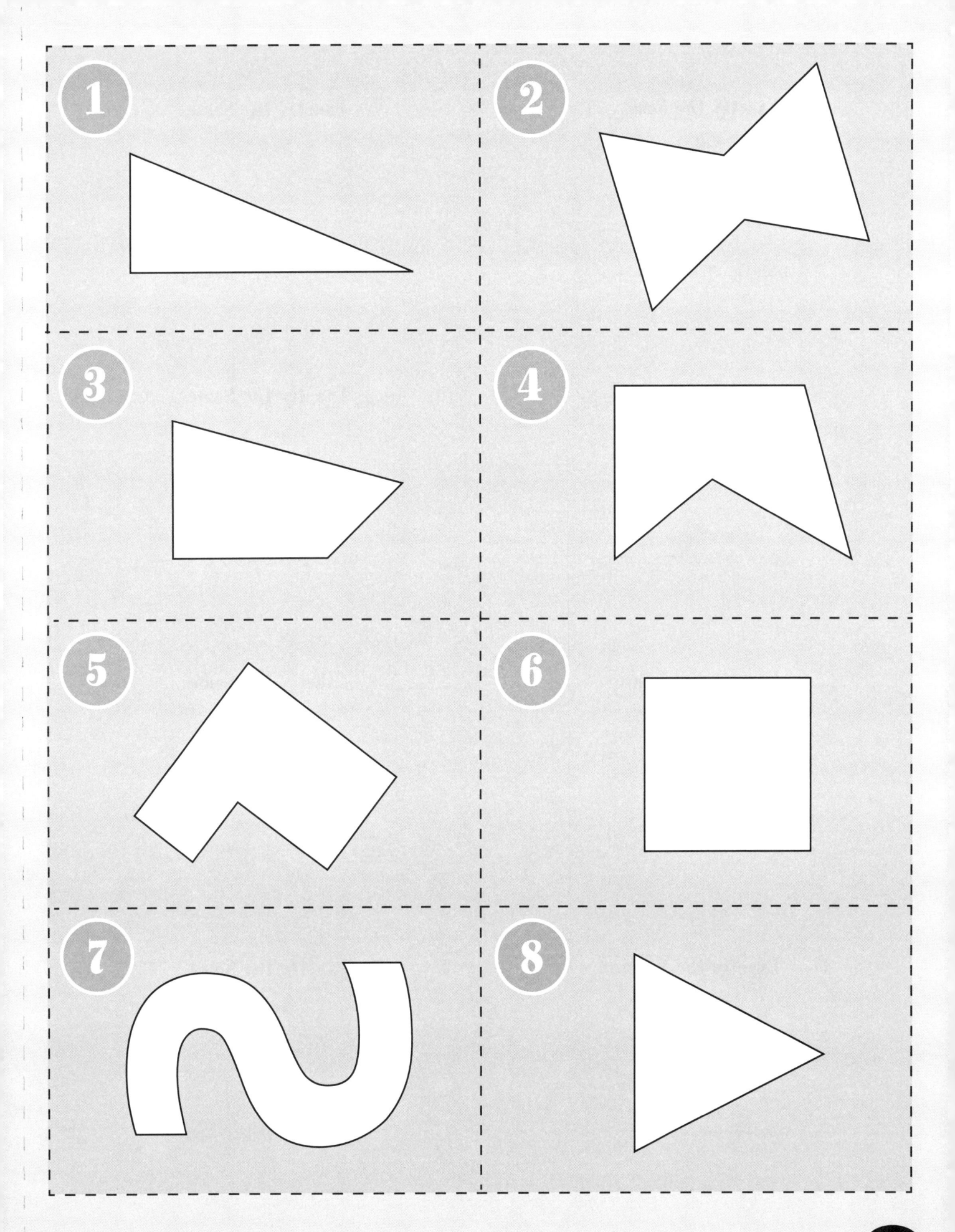

Exactly the Same
Set 2

EMC 3021
©2004 by Evan-Moor Corp.

Exactly the Same
Set 2

EMC 3021
©2004 by Evan-Moor Corp.

Exactly the Same
Set 2

EMC 3021
©2004 by Evan-Moor Corp.

Exactly the Same
Set 2

EMC 3021
©2004 by Evan-Moor Corp.

Exactly the Same
Set 2

EMC 3021
©2004 by Evan-Moor Corp.

Exactly the Same
Set 2

EMC 3021
©2004 by Evan-Moor Corp.

Exactly the Same
Set 2

EMC 3021
©2004 by Evan-Moor Corp.

Exactly the Same
Set 2

EMC 3021
©2004 by Evan-Moor Corp.

9	10
11	12
13	14
15	16

©2004 by Evan-Moor Corp. • Math Centers—Take It to Your Seat • EMC 3021

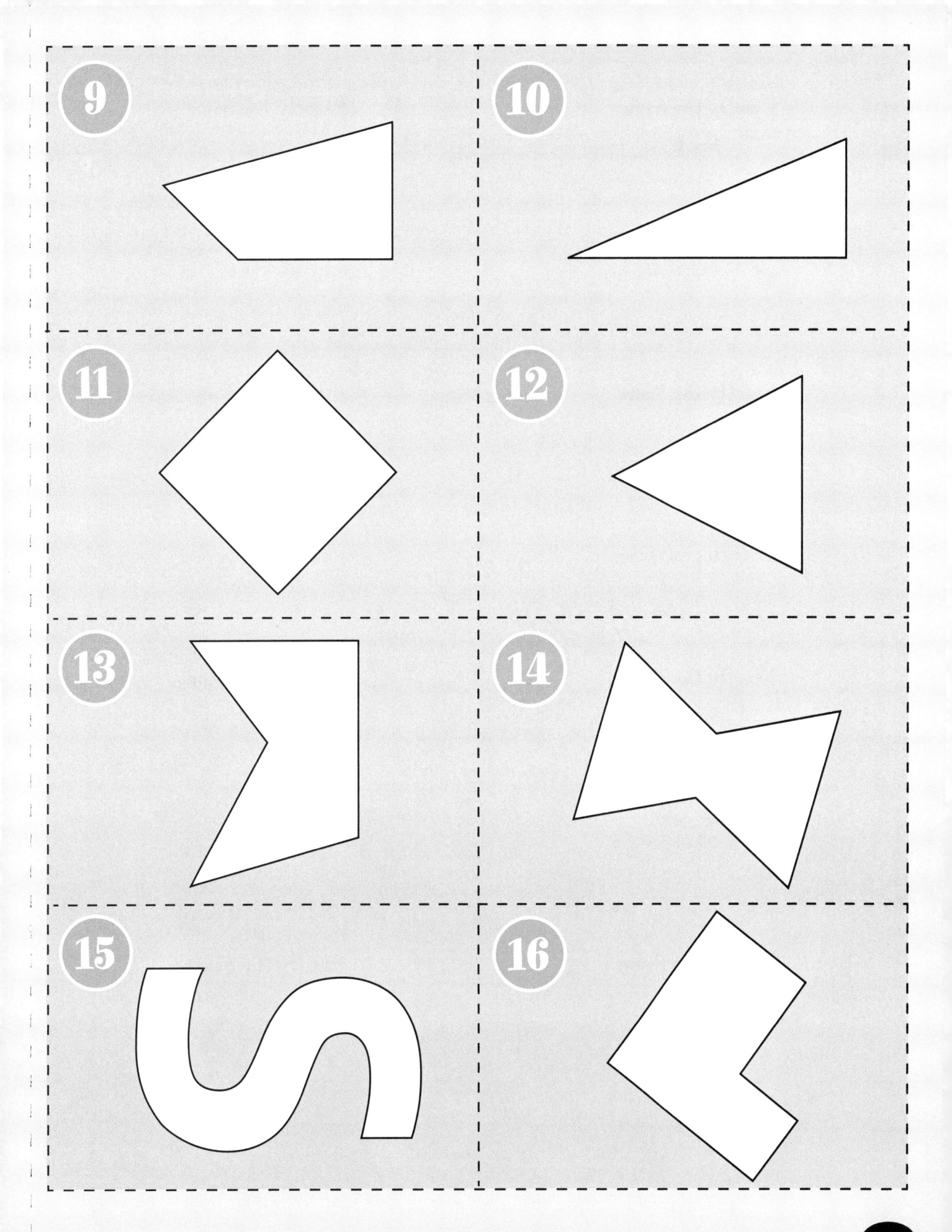

Exactly the Same
Set 2

EMC 3021
©2004 by Evan-Moor Corp.

Exactly the Same
Set 2

EMC 3021
©2004 by Evan-Moor Corp.

Exactly the Same
Set 2

EMC 3021
©2004 by Evan-Moor Corp.

Exactly the Same
Set 2

EMC 3021
©2004 by Evan-Moor Corp.

Exactly the Same
Set 2

EMC 3021
©2004 by Evan-Moor Corp.

Exactly the Same
Set 2

EMC 3021
©2004 by Evan-Moor Corp.

Exactly the Same
Set 2

EMC 3021
©2004 by Evan-Moor Corp.

Exactly the Same
Set 2

EMC 3021
©2004 by Evan-Moor Corp.

Money Machines

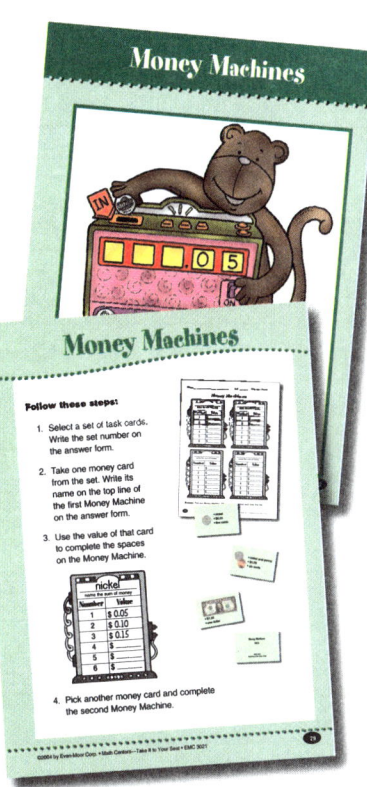

Preparing the Center

1. Prepare a folder following the directions on page 3.

   Cover—page 77
   Student Directions—page 79
   Task Cards—page 81

2. Reproduce a supply of the answer form on page 76. Place copies in the left-hand pocket of the folder.

Using the Center

1. The student selects a set of task cards and writes the set number on the answer form.

2. Next, the student takes one money card and writes its name at the top of a Money Machine. The student writes the value of the money card in the first row.

3. Using addition or multiplication, the student finds the value of two money cards and writes that amount in the second row. The student continues filling in each row to show how much money is in the machine.

4. Finally, the student selects a second money card and completes another Money Machine.

©2004 by Evan-Moor Corp. • Math Centers—Take It to Your Seat • EMC 3021

Name _____   Set _____   **Answer Form**

Money Machines

name the sum of money

Number	Value
1	$___.___
2	$___.___
3	$___.___
4	$___.___
5	$___.___
6	$___.___

name the sum of money

Number	Value
1	$___.___
2	$___.___
3	$___.___
4	$___.___
5	$___.___
6	$___.___

name the sum of money

Number	Value
1	$___.___
2	$___.___
3	$___.___
4	$___.___
5	$___.___
6	$___.___

name the sum of money

Number	Value
1	$___.___
2	$___.___
3	$___.___
4	$___.___
5	$___.___
6	$___.___

Bonus: Pick one Money Machine. What change occurred each time that the sum of money was dropped into the machine?

Math Centers—Take It to Your Seat • EMC 3021 • ©2004 by Evan-Moor Corp.

Money Machines

Money Machines

Follow these steps:

1. Select a set of task cards. Write the set number on the answer form.

2. Take one money card from the set. Write its name on the top line of the first Money Machine on the answer form.

3. Use the value of that card to complete the spaces on the Money Machine.

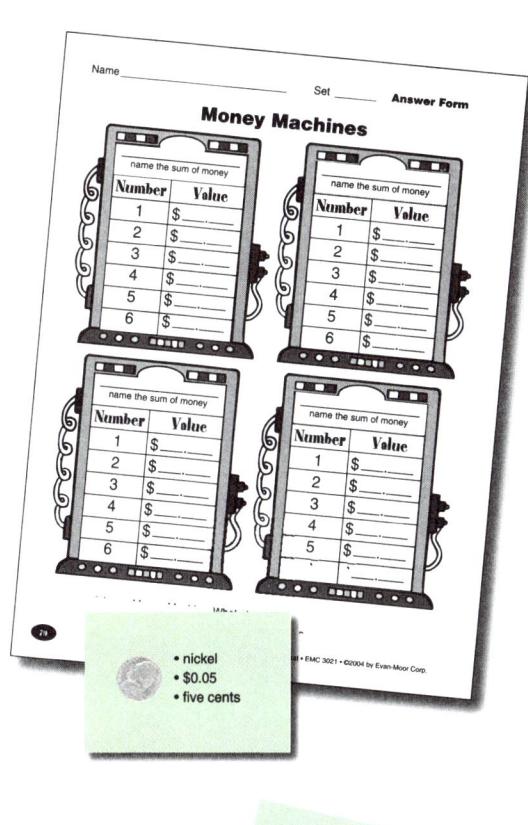

4. Pick another money card and complete the second Money Machine.

©2004 by Evan-Moor Corp. • Math Centers—Take It to Your Seat • EMC 3021

80

- nickel
- $0.05
- five cents

- dime
- $0.10
- ten cents

- nickel and penny
- $0.06
- six cents

- $1.00
- one dollar

- quarter
- $0.25
- twenty-five cents

- half dollar
- $0.50
- fifty cents

- $5.00
- five dollars

- one dollar and one nickel
- $1.05
- one dollar and five cents

Money Machines
Set 1

EMC 3021
©2004 by Evan-Moor Corp.

Money Machines
Set 1

EMC 3021
©2004 by Evan-Moor Corp.

Money Machines
Set 1

EMC 3021
©2004 by Evan-Moor Corp.

Money Machines
Set 1

EMC 3021
©2004 by Evan-Moor Corp.

Money Machines
Set 2

EMC 3021
©2004 by Evan-Moor Corp.

Money Machines
Set 2

EMC 3021
©2004 by Evan-Moor Corp.

Money Machines
Set 2

EMC 3021
©2004 by Evan-Moor Corp.

Money Machines
Set 2

EMC 3021
©2004 by Evan-Moor Corp.

Perimeter and Area

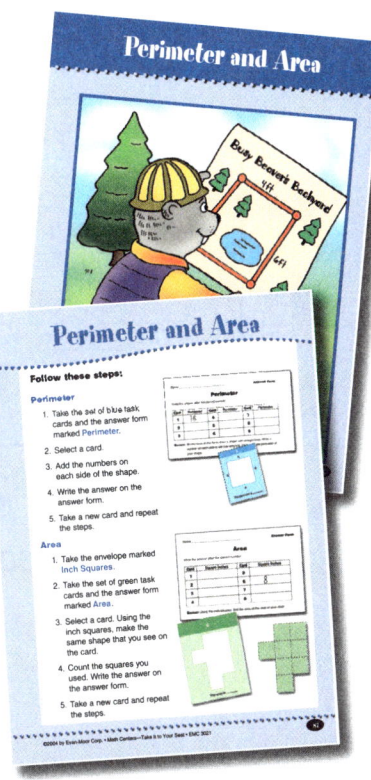

Preparing the Center

1. Prepare a folder following the directions on page 3.

   Cover—page 85
   Student Directions—page 87
   Task Cards—pages 89, 93, 95
   Inch Squares—page 91

2. Reproduce a supply of the answer forms on page 84. Place copies in the left-hand pocket of the folder.

Using the Center

1. The student selects a set of task cards and the correct answer form for that set.

2. If using the Perimeter set, the student adds the numbers marked on each shape to calculate the perimeter, and then writes the answers on the Perimeter answer form.

3. If using the Area set, the student uses the inch squares to copy each shape, and then counts the squares used and writes the answers on the Area answer form.

©2004 by Evan-Moor Corp. • Math Centers—Take It to Your Seat • EMC 3021

Name_____   **Answer Form**

Perimeter

Write the answer after the correct number.

Card	Perimeter	Card	Perimeter	Card	Perimeter
1		4		7	
2		5		8	
3		6		9	

Bonus: On the back of this form, draw a shape with straight lines. Write a number on each side to tell how long it is. Then write the perimeter of your shape.

Name_____   **Answer Form**

Area

Write the answer after the correct number.

Card	Square Inches	Card	Square Inches
1		5	
2		6	
3		7	
4		8	

Bonus: Using the inch squares, find the area of the seat of your chair.

Perimeter and Area

86

Perimeter and Area

Follow these steps:

Perimeter

1. Take the set of blue task cards and the answer form marked **Perimeter**.
2. Select a card.
3. Add the numbers on each side of the shape.
4. Write the answer on the answer form.
5. Take a new card and repeat the steps.

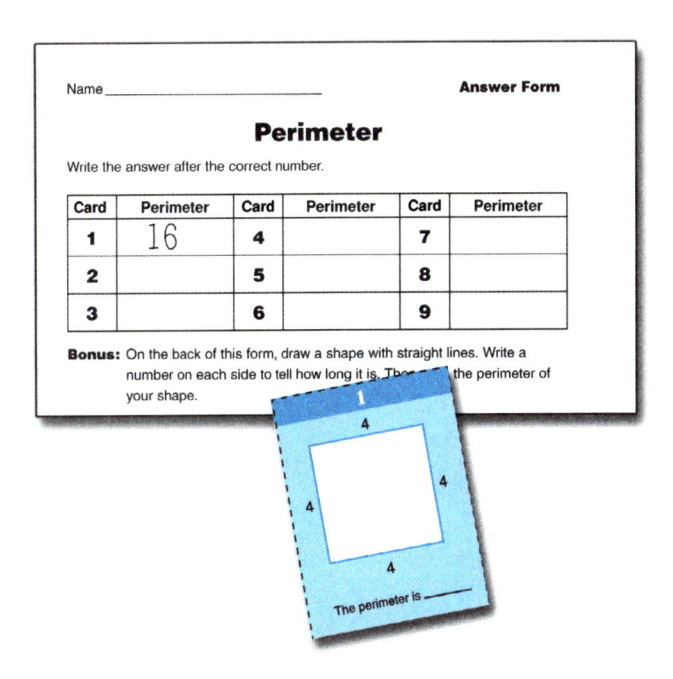

Area

1. Take the envelope marked **Inch Squares**.
2. Take the set of green task cards and the answer form marked **Area**.
3. Select a card. Using the inch squares, make the same shape that you see on the card.
4. Count the squares you used. Write the answer on the answer form.
5. Take a new card and repeat the steps.

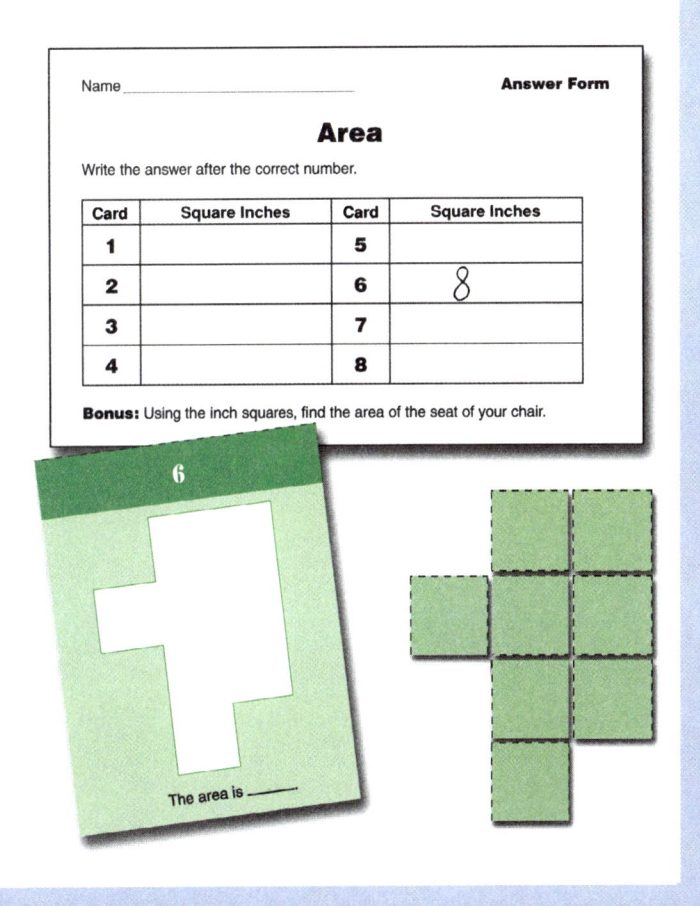

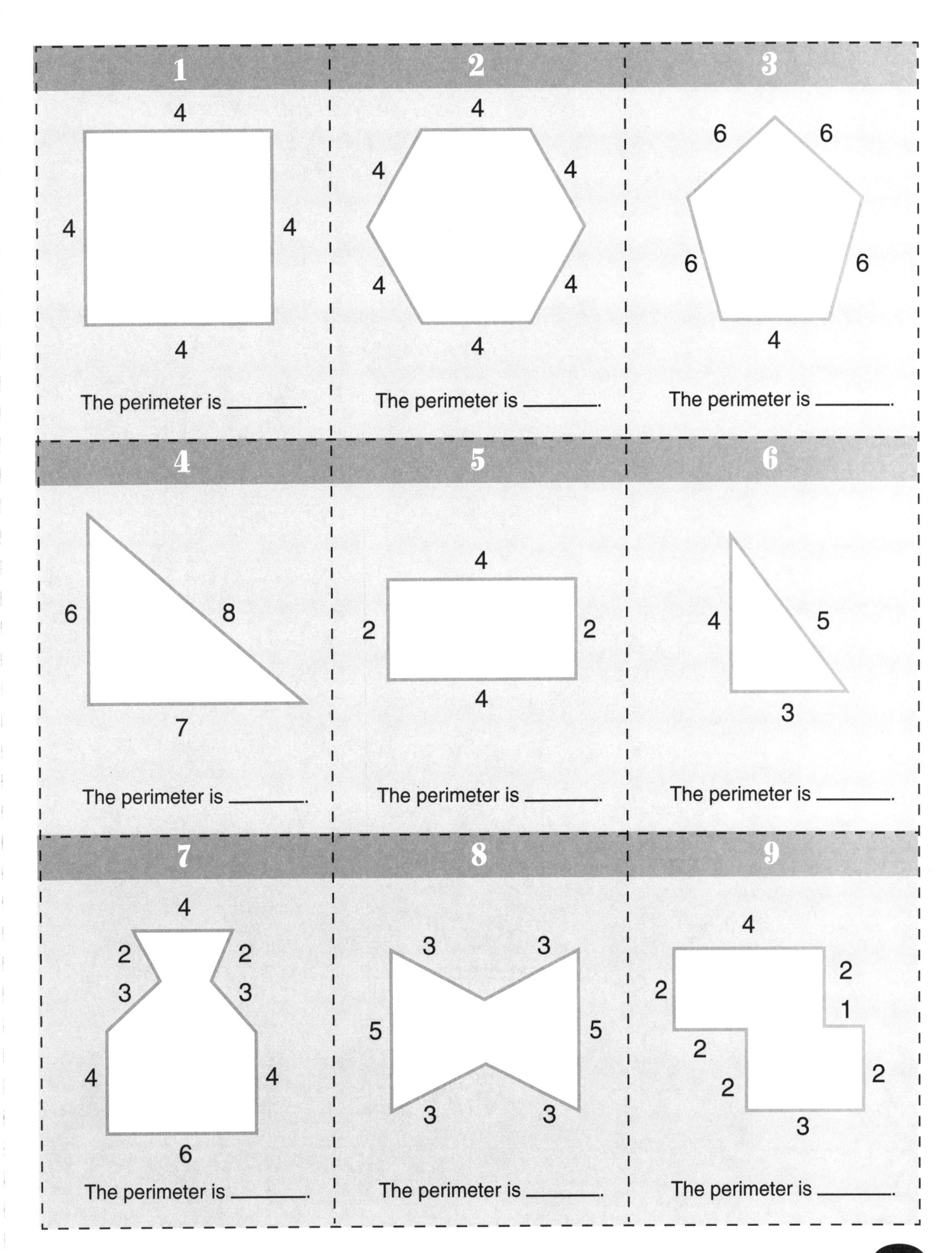

1

4, 4, 4, 4

The perimeter is _____.

2

4, 4, 4, 4, 4, 4

The perimeter is _____.

3

6, 6, 6, 6, 4

The perimeter is _____.

4

6, 8, 7

The perimeter is _____.

5

4, 2, 4, 2

The perimeter is _____.

6

4, 5, 3

The perimeter is _____.

7

4, 2, 2, 3, 3, 4, 4, 6

The perimeter is _____.

8

3, 3, 5, 5, 3, 3

The perimeter is _____.

9

4, 2, 1, 2, 2, 2, 3

The perimeter is _____.

Perimeter

EMC 3021
©2004 by Evan-Moor Corp.

Perimeter

EMC 3021
©2004 by Evan-Moor Corp.

Perimeter

EMC 3021
©2004 by Evan-Moor Corp.

Perimeter

EMC 3021
©2004 by Evan-Moor Corp.

Perimeter

EMC 3021
©2004 by Evan-Moor Corp.

Perimeter

EMC 3021
©2004 by Evan-Moor Corp.

Perimeter

EMC 3021
©2004 by Evan-Moor Corp.

Perimeter

EMC 3021
©2004 by Evan-Moor Corp.

Perimeter

EMC 3021
©2004 by Evan-Moor Corp.

©2004 by Evan-Moor Corp. • Math Centers—Take It to Your Seat • EMC 3021

1

The area is _____.

2

The area is _____.

3

The area is _____.

4

The area is _____.

Area

EMC 3021
©2004 by Evan-Moor Corp.

Area

EMC 3021
©2004 by Evan-Moor Corp.

Area

EMC 3021
©2004 by Evan-Moor Corp.

Area

EMC 3021
©2004 by Evan-Moor Corp.

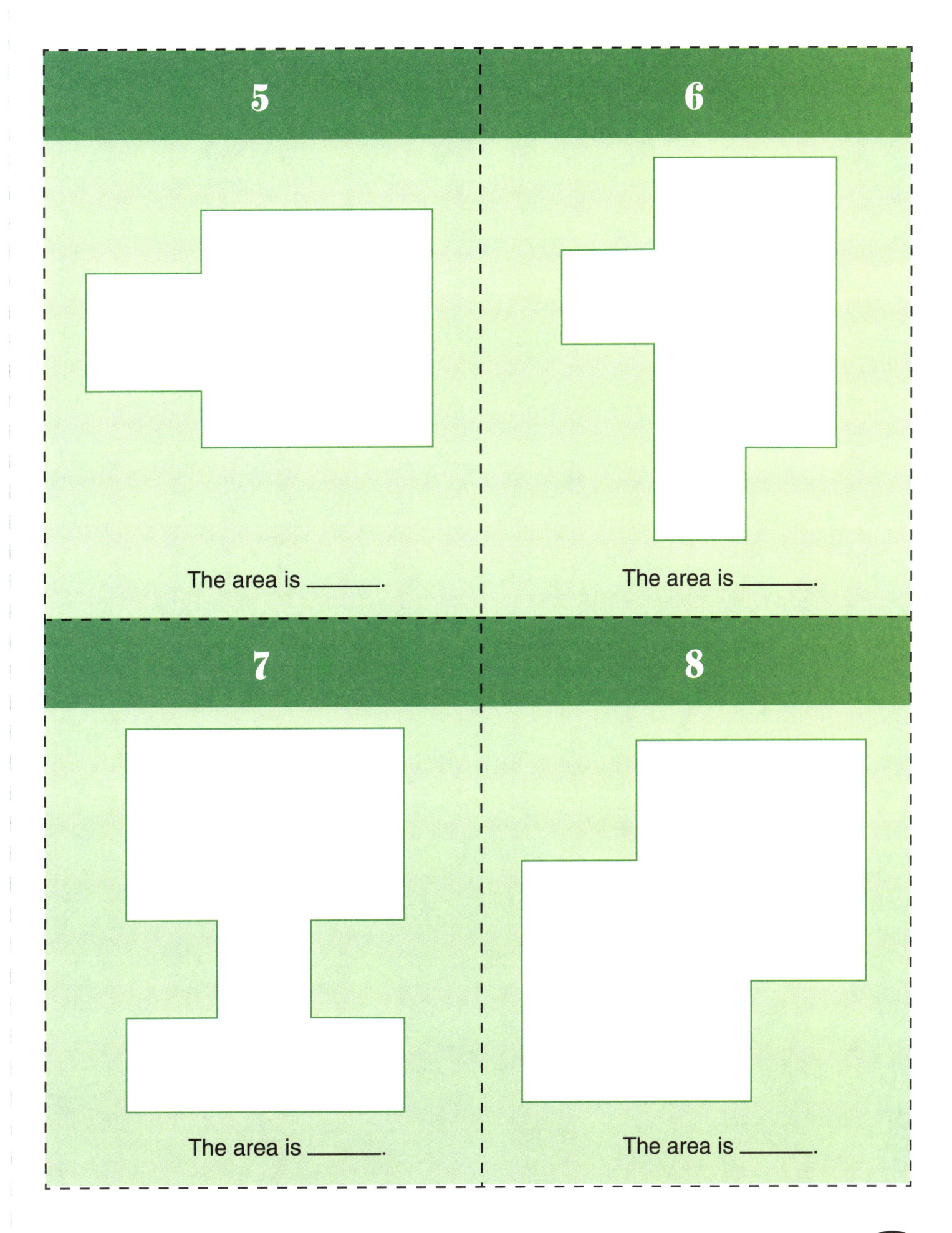

5

The area is _____.

6

The area is _____.

7

The area is _____.

8

The area is _____.

Area

EMC 3021
©2004 by Evan-Moor Corp.

Area

EMC 3021
©2004 by Evan-Moor Corp.

Area

EMC 3021
©2004 by Evan-Moor Corp.

Area

EMC 3021
©2004 by Evan-Moor Corp.

Measuring at the Circus

Preparing the Center

1. Prepare a folder following the directions on page 3.

   Cover—page 99
   Student Directions—page 101
   Rulers—page 103
   Task Cards—pages 105–111

2. Reproduce a supply of the answer form on page 98. Place copies in the left-hand pocket of the folder.

Using the Center

1. The student selects a task card and an answer form.

2. Next, the student reads the card, selects the correct ruler, and measures the pictures on the card. The student then writes the measurements on the answer form in the correct section.

3. The student repeats Step 2 to complete the remaining task cards.

©2004 by Evan-Moor Corp. • Math Centers—Take It to Your Seat • EMC 3021

Name_____   **Answer Form**

Measuring at the Circus

Measure the shape. Write the answer.

Card A
The Circus Clown
1. _____
2. _____
3. _____
4. _____

Card B
Circus Treats
1. _____
2. _____
3. _____
4. _____

Card C
Circus Animals
1. _____
2. _____
3. _____
4. _____

Card D
Around the Circus
1. _____
2. _____
3. _____
4. _____

Bonus: Trace your shoe on the back of this form. Measure it.

How long is it? _____   How wide is it? _____

Measuring at the Circus

100 Math Centers—Take It to Your Seat • EMC 3021 • ©2004 by Evan-Moor Corp.

Measuring at the Circus

Follow these steps:

1. Choose a task card and an answer form.

2. Read the questions on the card.

3. Take the correct ruler and measure the pictures.

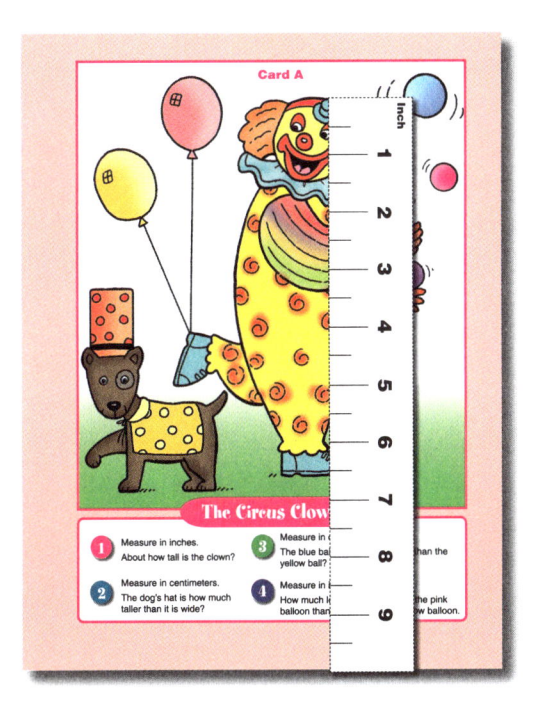

4. Write the answers on the answer form.

5. Repeat with the other cards.

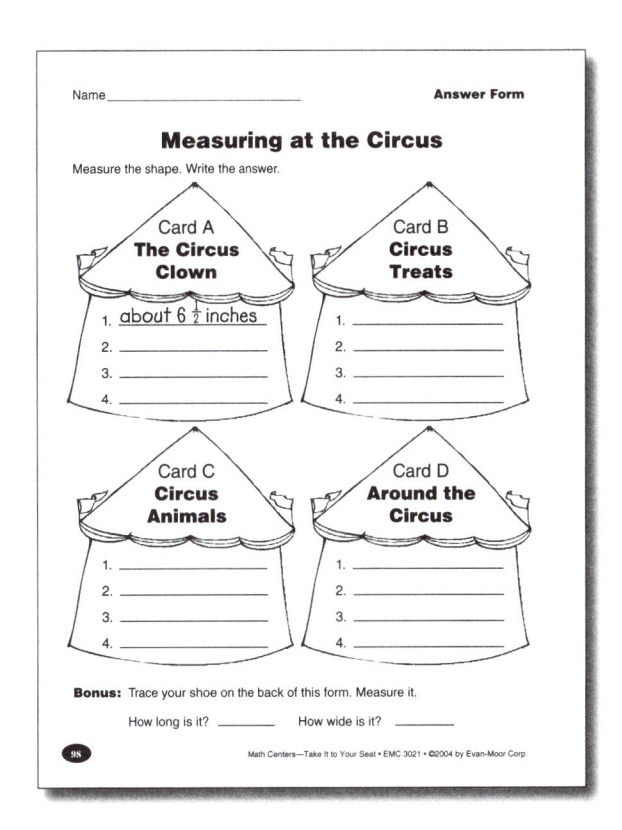

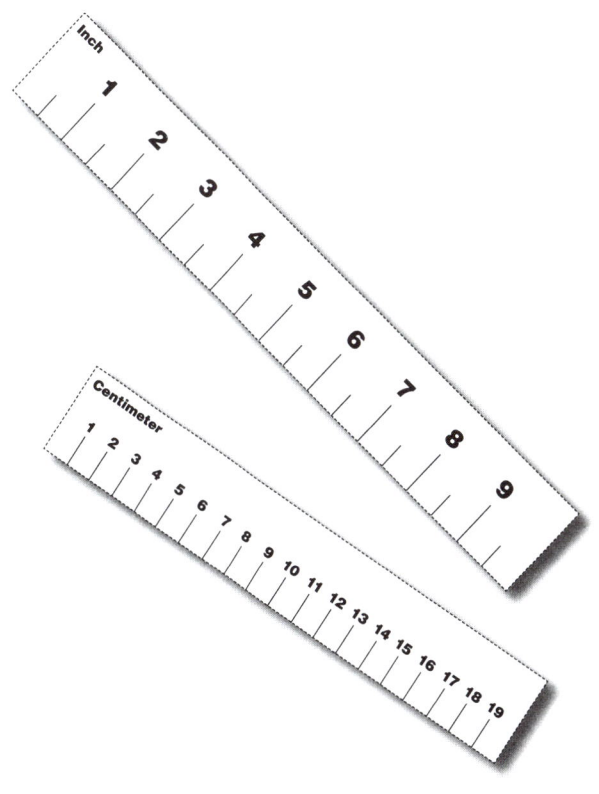

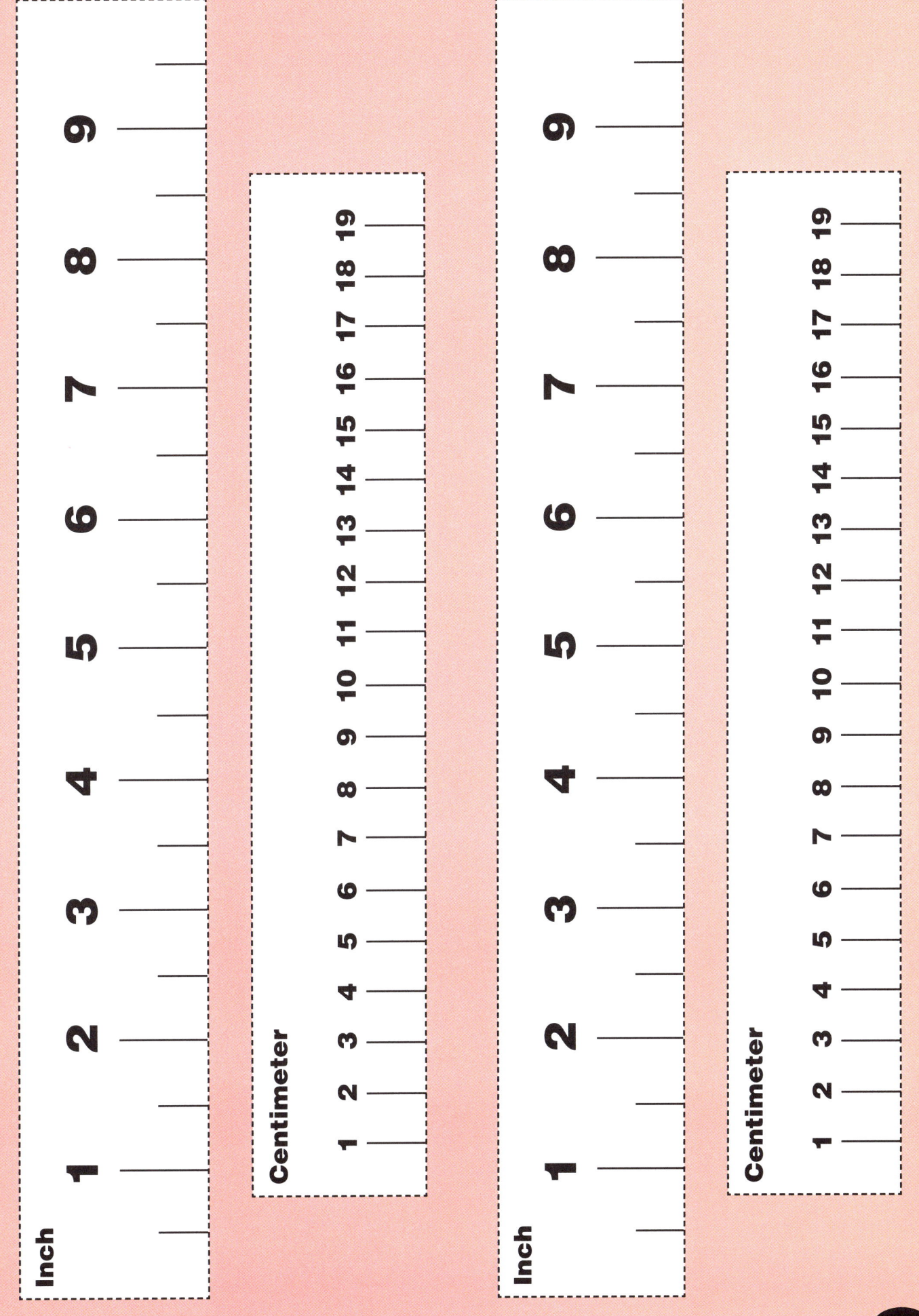

©2004 by Evan-Moor Corp. • Math Centers—Take It to Your Seat • EMC 3021

103

Card A

The Circus Clown

1 Measure in inches.
About how tall is the clown?

2 Measure in centimeters.
The dog's hat is how much taller than it is wide?

3 Measure in centimeters.
The blue ball is how much wider than the yellow ball?

4 Measure in inches.
How much longer is the string of the pink balloon than the string of the yellow balloon?

©2004 by Evan-Moor Corp. • Math Centers—Take It to Your Seat • EMC 3021

Measuring at the Circus
Card A

EMC 3021
©2004 by Evan-Moor Corp.

Card B

Circus Treats

1 Measure in centimeters.
How long is a peanut?

2 Measure in inches.
Without the popcorn, about how tall is the popcorn bag?

3 Measure in inches.
The candy stick is how much longer than it is wide?

4 Measure in centimeters.
Without the stick, the ice cream is how much taller than it is wide?

©2004 by Evan-Moor Corp. • Math Centers—Take It to Your Seat • EMC 3021

107

Measuring at the Circus

Card B

EMC 3021
©2004 by Evan-Moor Corp.

Card C

Welcome to the Circus

Circus Animals

1 Measure in inches.
How tall is the elephant?

2 Measure in centimeters.
The bear's bow is how much wider than the monkey's bow?

3 Measure in centimeters.
How much taller is the tallest dog than the middle dog?

4 Measure in inches.
Without the stick, the flag is how much longer than it is wide?

©2004 by Evan-Moor Corp. • Math Centers—Take It to Your Seat • EMC 3021

Measuring at the Circus

Card C

EMC 3021
©2004 by Evan-Moor Corp.

Card D

Around the Circus

1 Measure in centimeters.
How tall is the Master of Ceremonies?

2 Measure in inches.
How long is the yellow balance beam?

3 Measure in inches.
The base of the seal's stand is how much wider than the top of the stand?

4 Measure in inches and centimeters.
About how many inches wide is the trampoline? About how many centimeters wide is it?

©2004 by Evan-Moor Corp. • Math Centers—Take It to Your Seat • EMC 3021

Measuring at the Circus

Card D

EMC 3021
©2004 by Evan-Moor Corp.

Time Flies

Preparing the Center

1. Prepare a folder following the directions on page 3.

   Cover—page 115
   Student Directions—page 117
   Task Cards—pages 119–125

2. Reproduce a supply of the answer form on page 114. Place copies in the left-hand pocket of the folder.

Using the Center

1. The student selects a set of task cards and writes the set number on the answer form.

2. Next, the student reads the questions on the cards and writes the answers on the answer form.

3. The student draws the hands on the clockfaces for numbers 6 and 12 to show the answer.

©2004 by Evan-Moor Corp. • Math Centers—Take It to Your Seat • EMC 3021

113

Name_____   Set _____   **Answer Form**

Time Flies

Write the time after the number.
Show the time on the clockface.

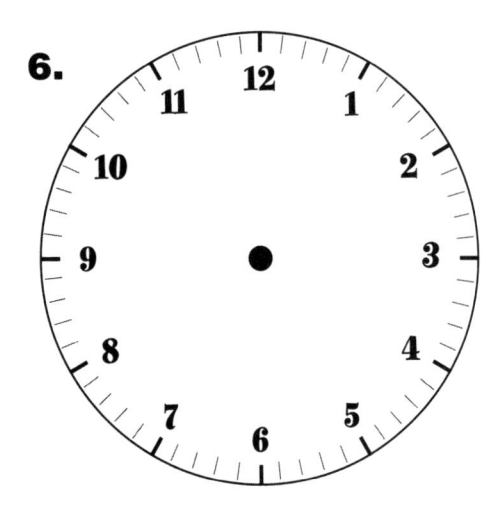

1. _____:_____   **7.** _____:_____

2. _____:_____   **8.** _____:_____

3. _____:_____   **9.** _____:_____

4. _____:_____   **10.** _____:_____

5. _____:_____   **11.** _____:_____

6.   **12.**

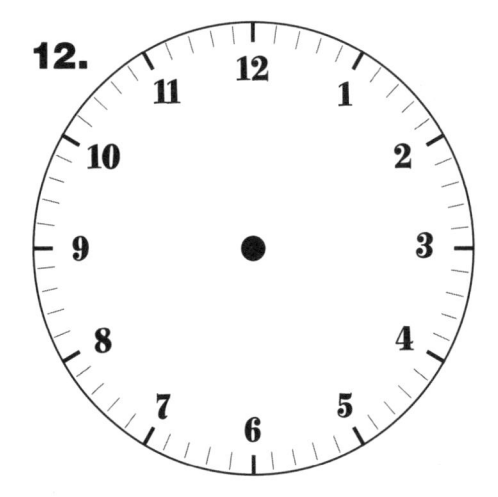

Bonus: Draw two clocks on the back of this form. Show the time that school starts. Show the time that school ends. How long are you in school each day?

Math Centers—Take It to Your Seat • EMC 3021 • ©2004 by Evan-Moor Corp.

Time Flies

Math Centers—Take It to Your Seat • EMC 3021 • ©2004 by Evan-Moor Corp.

Time Flies

Follow these steps:

1. Choose a set of task cards. Write the set number on the answer form.

2. Select a card and read the question.

3. Write the answer after the card's number on the answer form.

4. Repeat for the other cards. You will need to draw hands on the clockfaces to answer numbers 6 and 12.

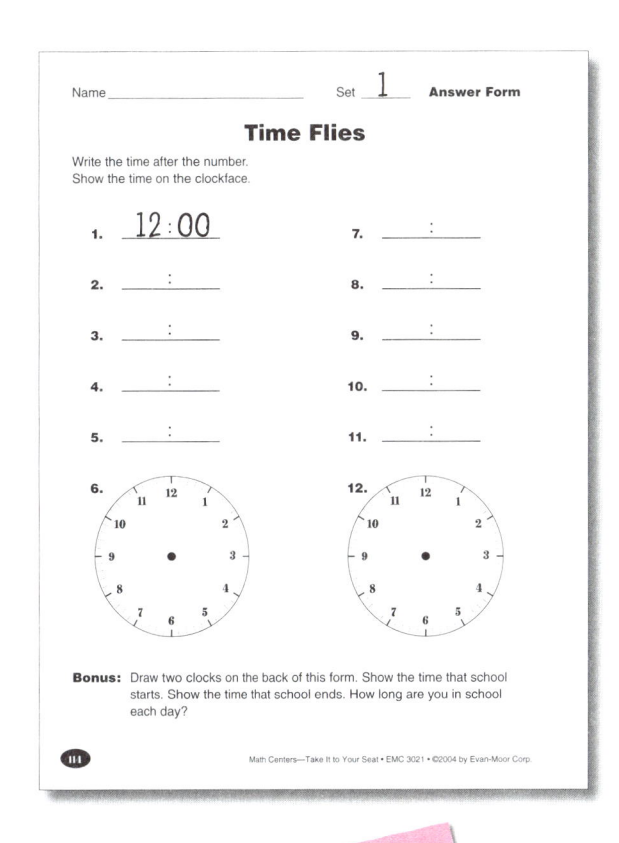

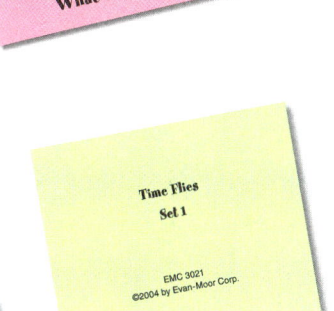

1

What time is it?

2

What time is it?

3

What time is it?

4

What time is it?

5

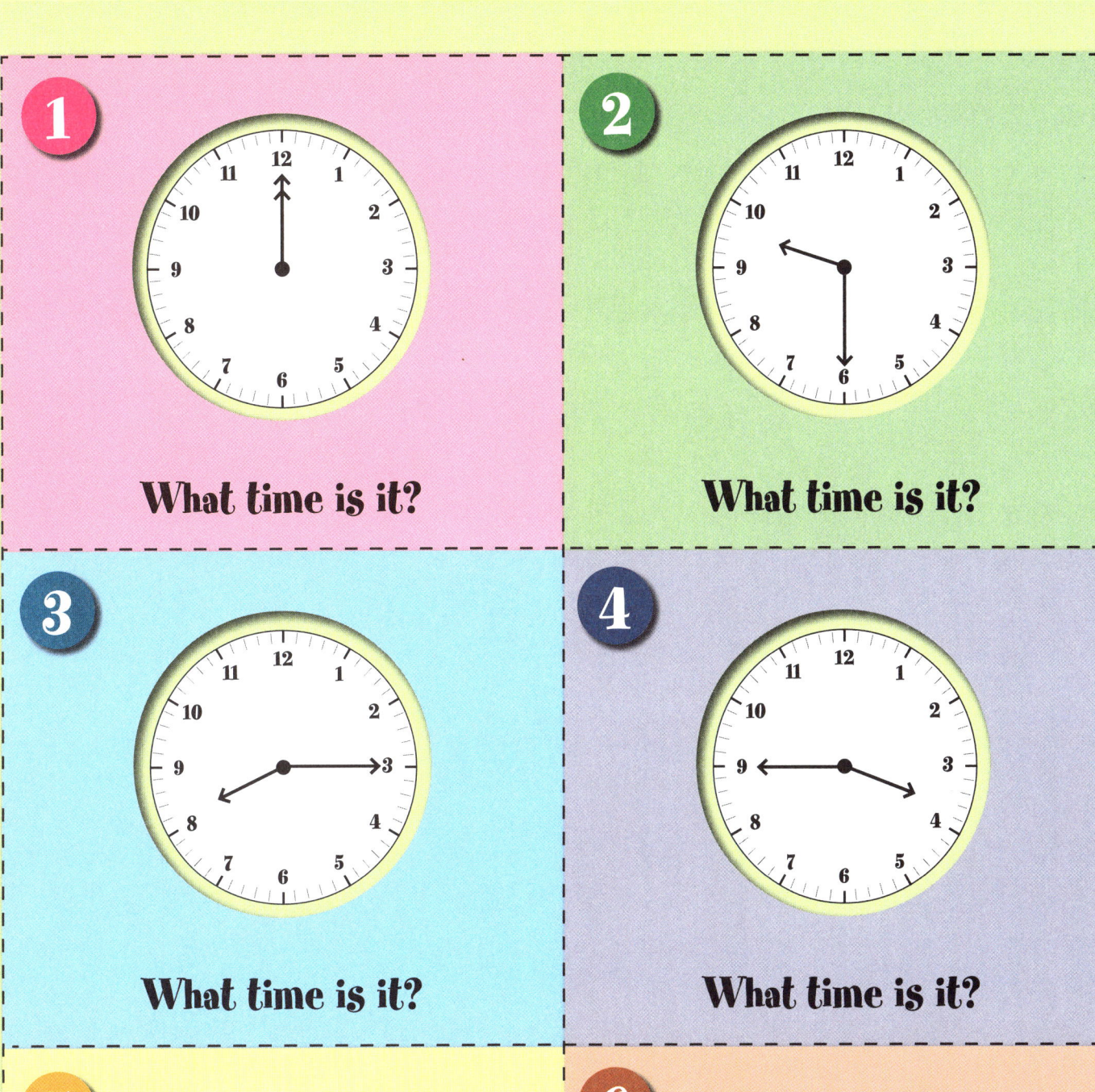

What time will it be in one hour?

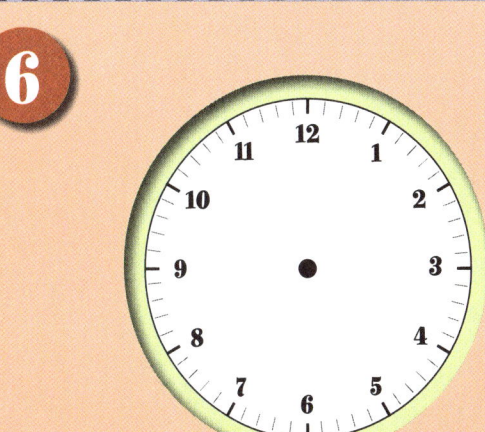

6

Make the clock show 11:30.

Time Flies
Set 1

EMC 3021
©2004 by Evan-Moor Corp.

Time Flies
Set 1

EMC 3021
©2004 by Evan-Moor Corp.

Time Flies
Set 1

EMC 3021
©2004 by Evan-Moor Corp.

Time Flies
Set 1

EMC 3021
©2004 by Evan-Moor Corp.

Time Flies
Set 1

EMC 3021
©2004 by Evan-Moor Corp.

Time Flies
Set 1

EMC 3021
©2004 by Evan-Moor Corp.

7 What time will it be in fifteen minutes?

8 What time was it one hour ago?

9 What time will it be in half an hour?

10 Sam's soccer game starts in one hour. It is now 2:30. At what time will the game start?

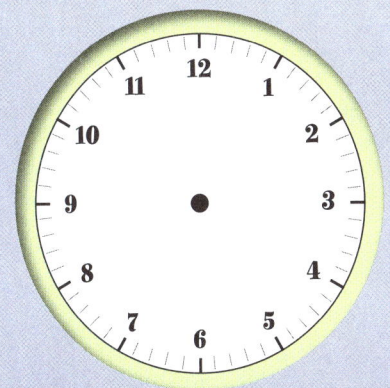

11 Ann is at the park. She has to be home by 3:15. It takes fifteen minutes to get to her house. At what time does she need to leave the park?

12 Make the clock show 5:15.

©2004 by Evan-Moor Corp. • Math Centers—Take It to Your Seat • EMC 3021

Time Flies

Set 1

EMC 3021
©2004 by Evan-Moor Corp.

Time Flies

Set 1

EMC 3021
©2004 by Evan-Moor Corp.

Time Flies

Set 1

EMC 3021
©2004 by Evan-Moor Corp.

Time Flies

Set 1

EMC 3021
©2004 by Evan-Moor Corp.

Time Flies

Set 1

EMC 3021
©2004 by Evan-Moor Corp.

Time Flies

Set 1

EMC 3021
©2004 by Evan-Moor Corp.

1

What time is it?

2

What time is it?

3

What time is it?

4

What time is it?

5

What time will it be in one hour?

6

Make the clock show 8:50.

Time Flies
Set 2

EMC 3021
©2004 by Evan-Moor Corp.

Time Flies
Set 2

EMC 3021
©2004 by Evan-Moor Corp.

Time Flies
Set 2

EMC 3021
©2004 by Evan-Moor Corp.

Time Flies
Set 2

EMC 3021
©2004 by Evan-Moor Corp.

Time Flies
Set 2

EMC 3021
©2004 by Evan-Moor Corp.

Time Flies
Set 2

EMC 3021
©2004 by Evan-Moor Corp.

7

What time will it be in five minutes?

8

What time was it thirty minutes ago?

9

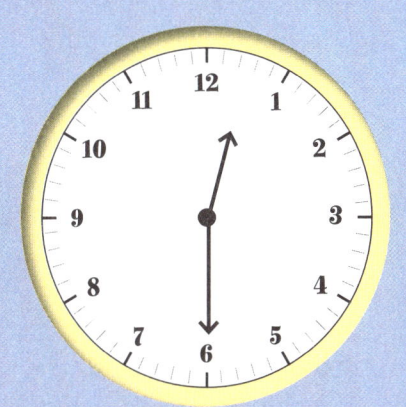

What time will it be in fifteen minutes?

10

Tanya started to clean her room at 10:15. She finished in an hour and five minutes. At what time did she finish?

11

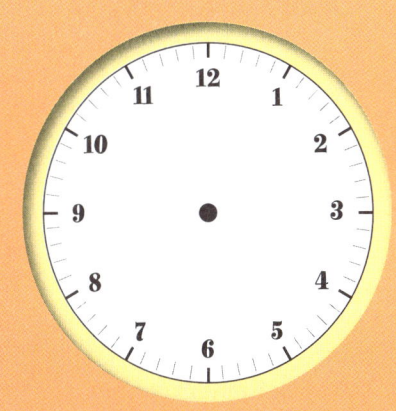

The football game began at 11:30. It lasted for three hours. At what time did the game end?

12

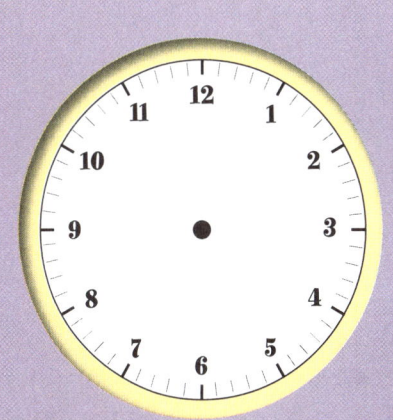

Make the clock show 5:17.

Time Flies
Set 2

EMC 3021
©2004 by Evan-Moor Corp.

Time Flies
Set 2

EMC 3021
©2004 by Evan-Moor Corp.

Time Flies
Set 2

EMC 3021
©2004 by Evan-Moor Corp.

Time Flies
Set 2

EMC 3021
©2004 by Evan-Moor Corp.

Time Flies
Set 2

EMC 3021
©2004 by Evan-Moor Corp.

Time Flies
Set 2

EMC 3021
©2004 by Evan-Moor Corp.

Read a Graph

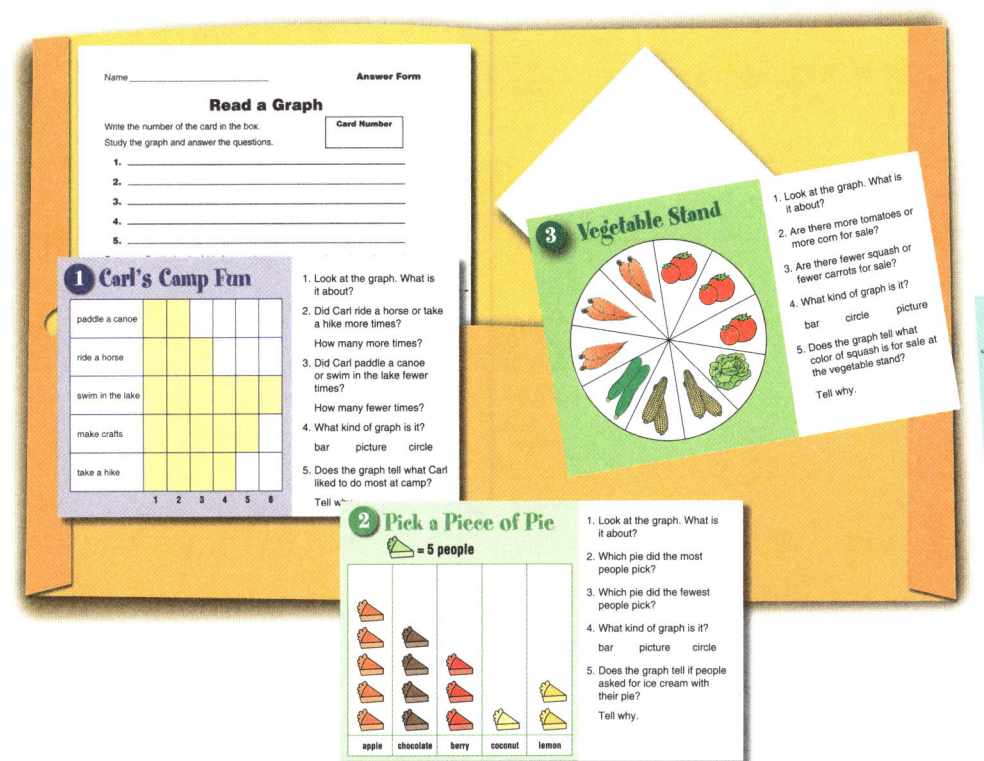

Preparing the Center

1. Prepare a folder following the directions on page 3.

    Cover—page 129
    Student Directions—page 131
    Task Cards—pages 133–137

2. Reproduce a supply of the answer form on page 128. Place copies in the left-hand pocket of the folder.

Using the Center

1. The student selects a task card and an answer form.

2. Next, the student studies the graph shown on the card.

3. Finally, the student answers questions relating to the graph.

4. If there is time, the student selects other cards and answer forms, and answers questions about those graphs.

©2004 by Evan-Moor Corp. • Math Centers—Take It to Your Seat • EMC 3021

127

Name _____ **Answer Form**

Read a Graph

Write the number of the card in the box.

Study the graph and answer the questions.

Card Number

1. _____

2. _____

3. _____

4. _____

5. _____

Bonus: On the back of this form, write two more questions about the graph. Write the answers to the questions.

- -

Name _____ **Answer Form**

Read a Graph

Write the number of the card in the box.

Study the graph and answer the questions.

Card Number

1. _____

2. _____

3. _____

4. _____

5. _____

Bonus: On the back of this form, write two more questions about the graph. Write the answers to the questions.

Read a Graph

130

Read a Graph

Follow these steps:

1. Pick a graph card. Write the number of the card in the box on the answer form.

2. Study the graph and read the questions.

3. Write the answers on the answer form.

4. Take another graph card and another answer form and repeat the steps.

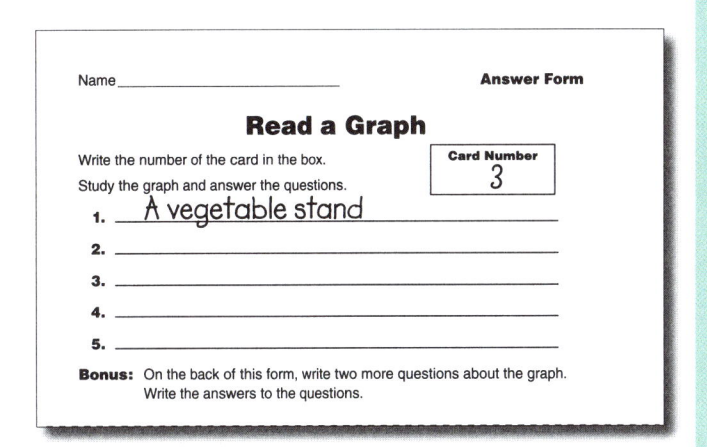

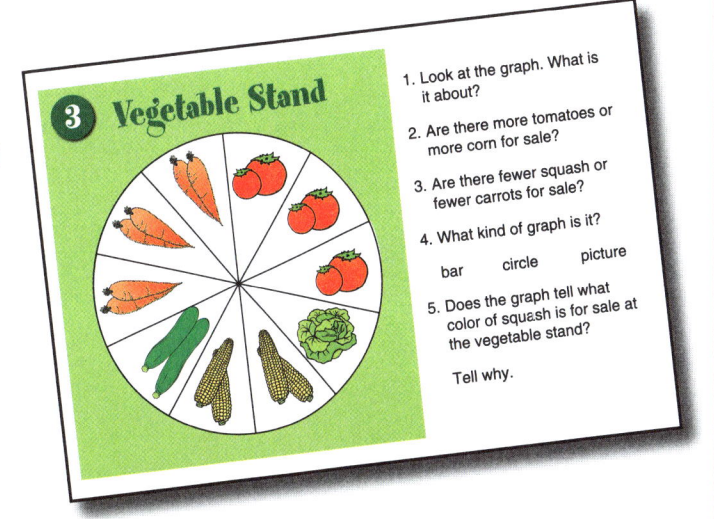

132 Math Centers—Take It to Your Seat • EMC 3021 • ©2004 by Evan-Moor Corp.

1 Carl's Camp Fun

	1	2	3	4	5	6
paddle a canoe	■	■				
ride a horse	■	■	■			
swim in the lake	■	■	■	■	■	■
make crafts	■	■	■	■		
take a hike	■	■	■	■	■	

1. Look at the graph. What is it about?
2. Did Carl ride a horse or take a hike more times?

   How many more times?
3. Did Carl paddle a canoe or swim in the lake fewer times?

   How many fewer times?
4. What kind of graph is it?

   bar   picture   circle
5. Does the graph tell what Carl liked to do most at camp?

   Tell why.

2 Pick a Piece of Pie

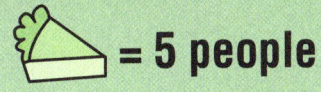

🥧 = 5 people

apple	chocolate	berry	coconut	lemon
5	4	3	2	2

1. Look at the graph. What is it about?
2. Which pie did the most people pick?
3. Which pie did the fewest people pick?
4. What kind of graph is it?

   bar   picture   circle
5. Does the graph tell if people asked for ice cream with their pie?

   Tell why.

©2004 by Evan-Moor Corp. • Math Centers—Take It to Your Seat • EMC 3021

Read a Graph

EMC 3021
©2004 by Evan-Moor Corp.

Read a Graph

EMC 3021
©2004 by Evan-Moor Corp.

3 Vegetable Stand

1. Look at the graph. What is it about?

2. Are there more tomatoes or more corn for sale?

3. Are there fewer squash or fewer carrots for sale?

4. What kind of graph is it?

    bar   circle   picture

5. Does the graph tell what color of squash is for sale at the vegetable stand?

    Tell why.

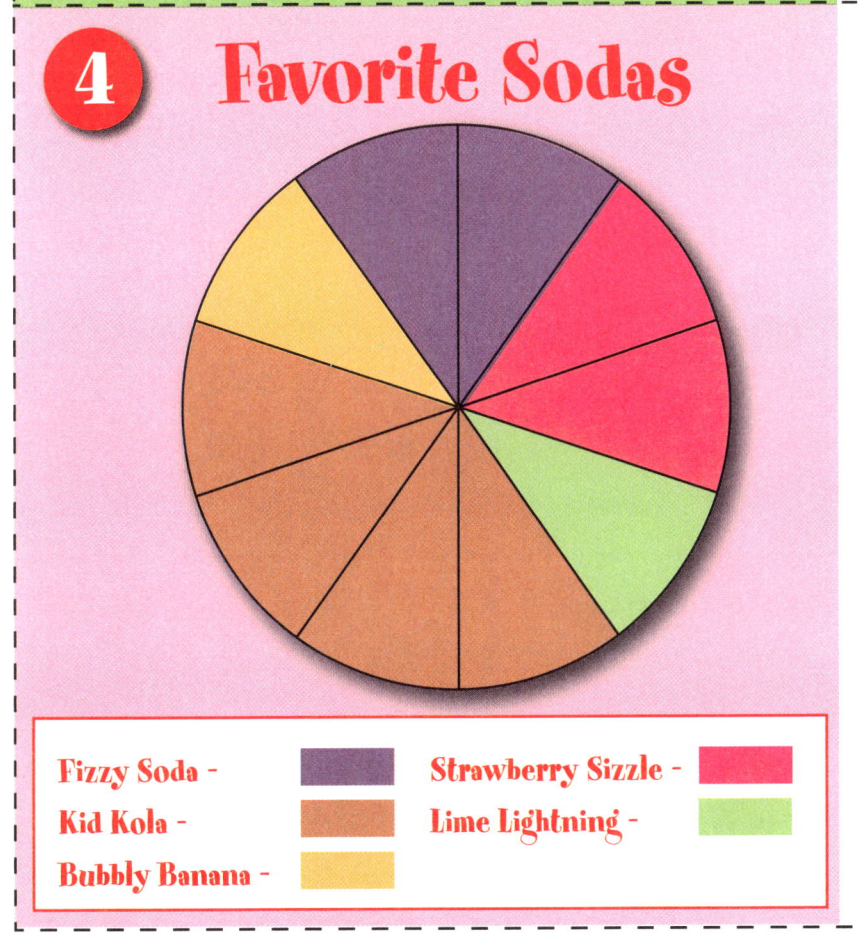

4 Favorite Sodas

1. Look at the graph. What is it about?

2. How many different kinds of soda are shown on the graph?

3. Which soda is the favorite?

4. What kind of graph is it?

    bar   circle   picture

5. Does the graph tell how many people like Pink Lemonade?

    Tell why.

Fizzy Soda -
Kid Kola -
Bubbly Banana -
Strawberry Sizzle -
Lime Lightning -

©2004 by Evan-Moor Corp. • Math Centers—Take It to Your Seat • EMC 3021

Read a Graph

EMC 3021
©2004 by Evan-Moor Corp.

Read a Graph

EMC 3021
©2004 by Evan-Moor Corp.

5 Number of Books George Checked Out

📘 = 2 Books

January: 📘📘
February: 📘📘 📘
March: 📘
April: 📘📘📘📘
May: 📘📘📘
June: 📘📘📘📘📘📘

1. Look at the graph. What is it about?

2. How many books did George check out in February?

3. In which month did George check out the most books?

4. What kind of graph is it?

   bar   circle   picture

5. Does the graph tell why George checked out so many books in June?

   Tell why.

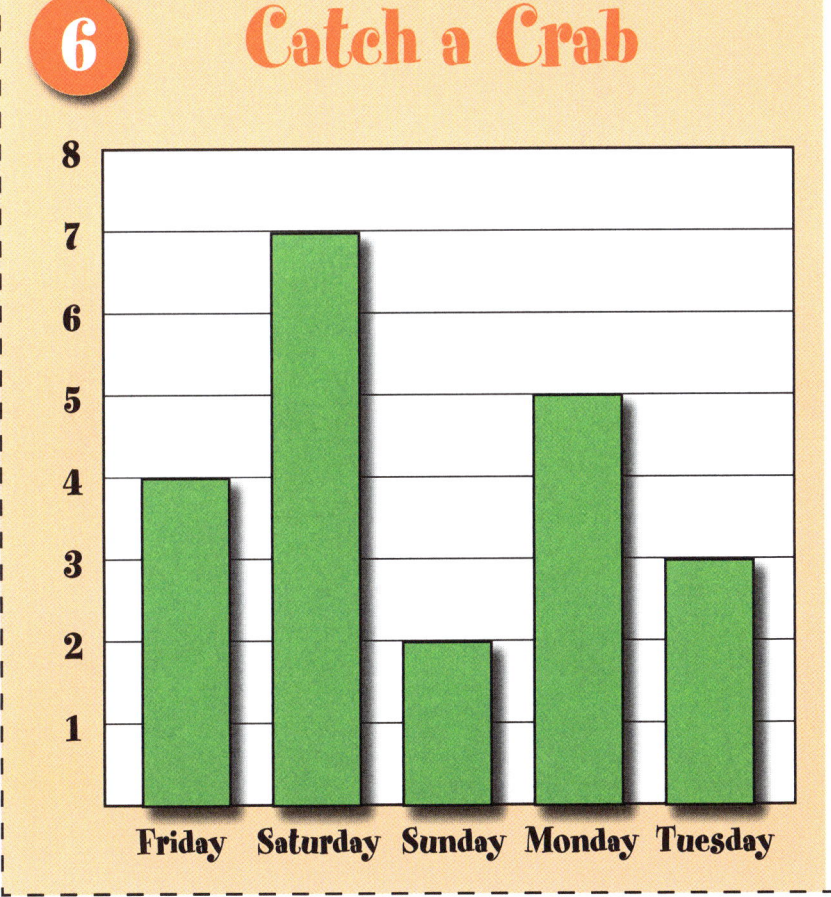

6 Catch a Crab

Friday: 4
Saturday: 7
Sunday: 2
Monday: 5
Tuesday: 3

1. Look at the graph. What is it about?

2. Were more crabs caught on Saturday or on Tuesday?

   How many more?

3. How many crabs were caught in all?

4. What kind of graph is it?

   bar   circle   picture

5. Does the graph tell how many crabs were caught on Thursday?

   Tell why.

©2004 by Evan-Moor Corp. • Math Centers—Take It to Your Seat • EMC 3021

Read a Graph

EMC 3021
©2004 by Evan-Moor Corp.

Read a Graph

EMC 3021
©2004 by Evan-Moor Corp.

Make a Graph

Preparing the Center

1. Prepare a folder following the directions on page 3.

   Cover—page 143
   Student Directions—page 145
   Task Cards—pages 147, 149

2. Reproduce a supply of the answer forms on pages 140–142. Place copies in the left-hand pocket of the folder.

Using the Center

1. The student selects a set of task cards.

2. Next, the student takes a card. After reading the card, the student selects the correct graph form and writes the set number and card number on the answer form.

3. The student creates a graph using the information on the card.

4. If there is time, the student selects another card and answer form, and creates a second graph.

©2004 by Evan-Moor Corp. • Math Centers—Take It to Your Seat • EMC 3021

139

Name _____ Set _____ Card _____ **Answer Form**

Make a Graph

Bar Graph

_____
graph title

12					
11					
10					
9					
8					
7					
6					
5					
4					
3					
2					
1					

_____ _____ _____ _____ _____

Bonus: On the back of this form, write three questions about the graph. Write the answers to the questions.

140   Math Centers—Take It to Your Seat • EMC 3021 • ©2004 by Evan-Moor Corp.

Name _____ Set _____ Card _____ **Answer Form**

Make a Graph
Picture Graph

_____
graph title

_____
_____
_____
_____
_____
_____

Bonus: On the back of this form, write three questions about the graph. Write the answers to the questions.

©2004 by Evan-Moor Corp. • Math Centers—Take It to Your Seat • EMC 3021

141

Name _____ Set _____ Card _____ **Answer Form**

Make a Graph
Circle Graph

_____
graph title

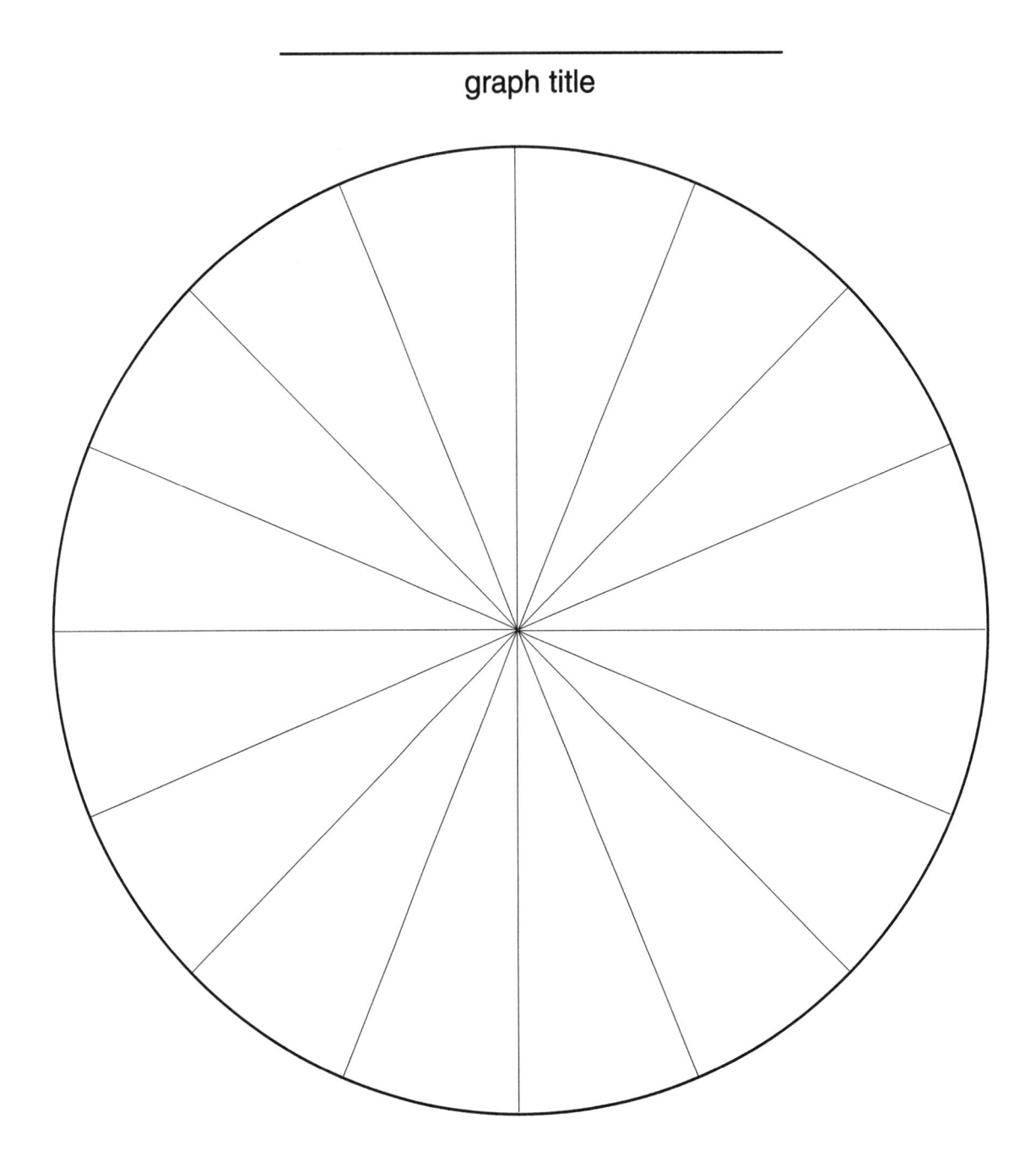

Bonus: On the back of this form, write three questions about the graph. Write the answers to the questions.

Make a Graph

Make a Graph

Follow these steps:

1. Take a set of task cards and pick a card.

2. Read the card, and then take the correct graph form. Write the set number and the card number on the form.

3. Use the information on the card to make a graph.

4. If there is time, pick a new card and answer form and make another graph.

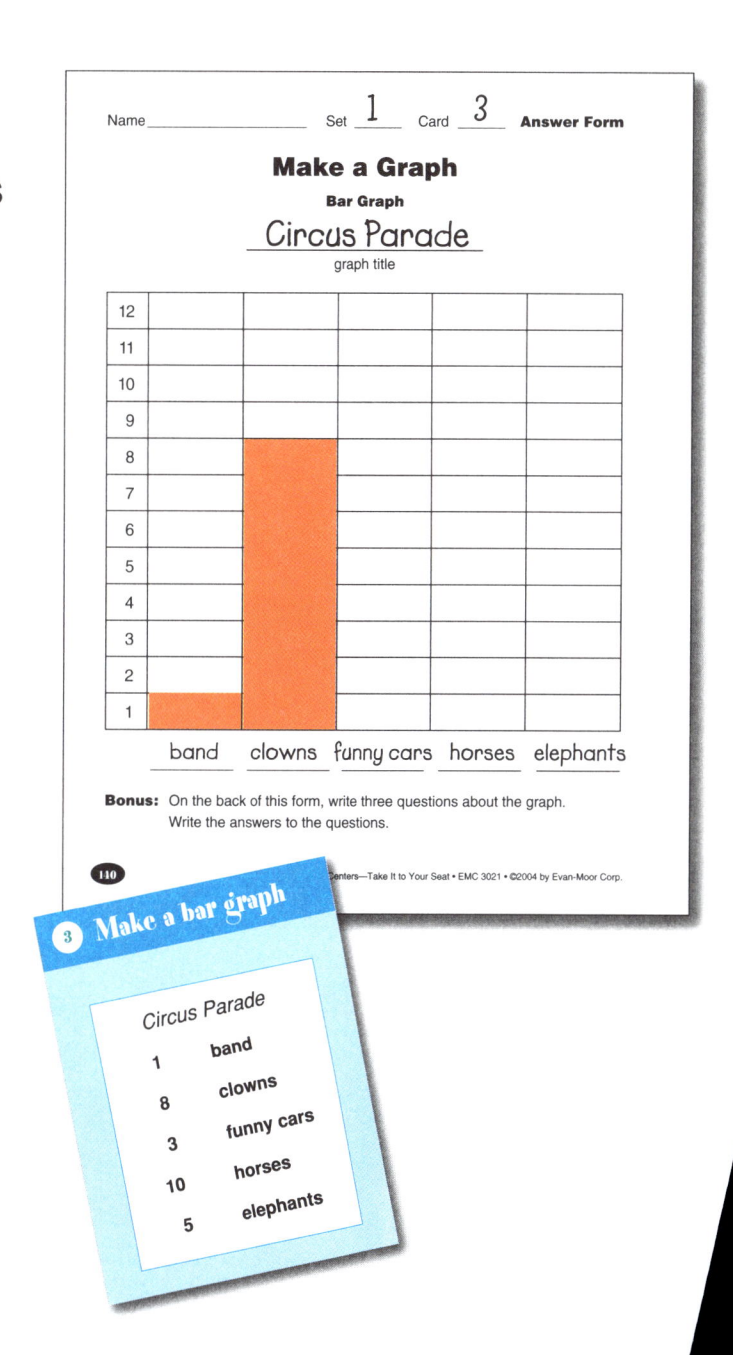

©2004 by Evan-Moor Corp. • Math Centers—Take It to Your Seat • EMC 3021

145

① Make a picture graph

Choosing Fruit

6 🍎   12 🍇

10 🍊   7 🟣

3 🍌   4 🍑

② Make a bar graph

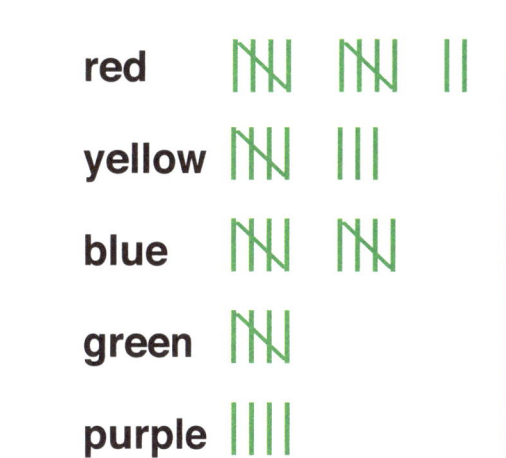

Favorite Colors

red   𝍫𝍫 𝍫𝍫 ||
yellow   𝍫𝍫 |||
blue   𝍫𝍫 𝍫𝍫
green   𝍫𝍫
purple ||||

③ Make a bar graph

Circus Parade

1   band
8   clowns
3   funny cars
10   horses
5   elephants

④ Make a bar graph

What Did You Drink for Lunch?

milk   𝍫𝍫 𝍫𝍫 ||
juice   𝍫𝍫 𝍫𝍫
water |||
chocolate milk   𝍫𝍫 ||
tea ||

©2004 by Evan-Moor Corp. • Math Centers—Take It to Your Seat • EMC 3021

Make a Graph

Set 1

EMC 3021
©2004 by Evan-Moor Corp.

Make a Graph

Set 1

EMC 3021
©2004 by Evan-Moor Corp.

Make a Graph

Set 1

EMC 3021
©2004 by Evan-Moor Corp.

Make a Graph

Set 1

EMC 3021
©2004 by Evan-Moor Corp.

① Ben's Graph

Last week, Ben counted ducks at the pond near his house. He made a tally as he counted.

Sunday	IIII IIII IIII IIII
Monday	IIII IIII
Tuesday	IIII IIII IIII
Wednesday	IIII
Thursday	IIII
Friday	IIII IIII IIII IIII IIII

He made a picture graph to show how many ducks he counted. Each duck on his graph counts as 5 ducks. He named the graph Ducks at the Pond.

② Betty's Graph

Betty took cookies to a picnic. She counted the different cookies that were eaten.

	chocolate chip cookies	8
	peanut butter cookies	3
	sugar cookies	1
	gingerbread cookies	4

She made a circle graph about the cookies. She named the graph Cookies.

③ Raul's Graph

Raul counted the pets in his neighborhood. He made a chart as he counted.

dogs	IIII IIII
cats	IIII IIII
fish	III
rabbits	II
hamsters	IIII

Then Raul made a bar graph to show the pets. He named it Pets in My Neighborhood.

④ Marina's Graph

Marina counted 5 girls and 3 boys with blond hair. She counted 4 boys with brown hair. There were 2 boys and 1 girl with black hair, and 1 boy with red hair. She made a circle graph showing the hair color of kids in her class. She named it Hair Color.

©2004 by Evan-Moor Corp. • MATH CENTERS—Take It to Your Seat • EMC 3021

Make a Graph
Set 2

EMC 3021
©2004 by Evan-Moor Corp.

Make a Graph
Set 2

EMC 3021
©2004 by Evan-Moor Corp.

Make a Graph
Set 2

EMC 3021
©2004 by Evan-Moor Corp.

Make a Graph
Set 2

EMC 3021
©2004 by Evan-Moor Corp.

Name That Shape!

Preparing the Center

1. Prepare a folder following the directions on page 3.

   Cover—page 153
   Student Directions—page 155
   Task Cards—pages 157–167

2. Reproduce a supply of the answer forms on page 152. Place copies in the left-hand pocket of the folder.

Using the Center

1. The student selects a set of task cards and takes the correct answer form.

2. Next, the student matches the cards—by shape, the shape's name, and the shape's attributes.

3. On the Set 1 answer form, the student draws the shape, writes its name, and writes the number of the correct attribute card.

   On the Set 2 answer form, the student writes the name of the shape and the number of the correct attribute card.

©2004 by Evan-Moor Corp. • Math Centers—Take It to Your Seat • EMC 3021

Name _____

Set 1   Answer Form

Name That Shape!

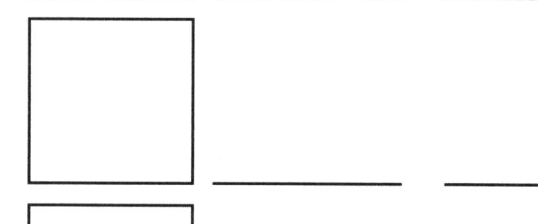

Draw the shape	Write its name	Write the number of the attribute card
☐	_____	_____
☐	_____	_____
☐	_____	_____
☐	_____	_____
☐	_____	_____
☐	_____	_____

Bonus: Draw a shape that has these attributes:
- eight straight sides
- all sides the same length

Name the shape you draw.

Name _____

Set 2   Answer Form

Name That Shape!

	Write its name	Write the number of the attribute card
 sphere	_____	_____
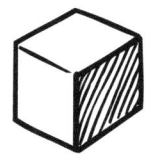 cube	_____	_____
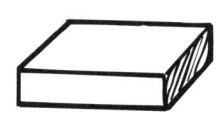 rectangular prism	_____	_____
 cone	_____	_____
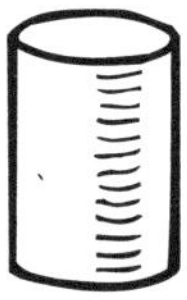 cylinder	_____	_____
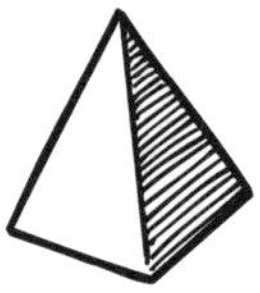 pyramid	_____	_____

Bonus: Draw a shape that has these attributes:
- eight straight sides
- all sides the same length

Name the shape you draw.

152   Math Centers—Take It to Your Seat • EMC 3021 • ©2004 by Evan-Moor Corp.

Name That Shape!

- What has four sides and four corners? All sides are the same.
- What has three sides and three corners?
- What has 4 sides. 2 long...
- What has 6 sides and 6 corners?
- What is a closed curve with no corners?

©2004 by Evan-Moor Corp. • Math Centers—Take It to Your Seat • EMC 3021

153

Name That Shape!

Follow these steps:

1. Choose a set of task cards. Choose the correct answer form.
2. Match the cards to make sets of three.

   shape card   **name card**    **attribute card**

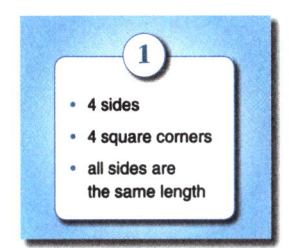

   square

   - 4 sides
   - 4 square corners
   - all sides are the same length

3. For Set 1 only, draw the shape on the answer form.
4. Write the shape's name on the answer form.
5. Write the number of the attribute card on the answer form.

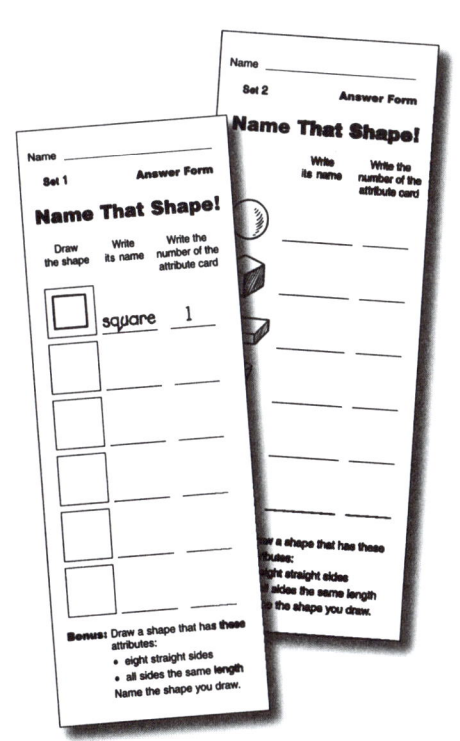

Terms to know:

Set 1 — corner, side

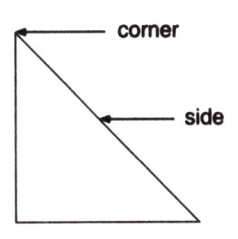

Set 2 — edge, vertex, side

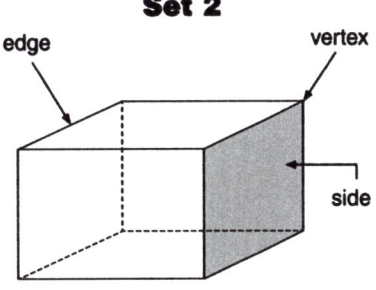

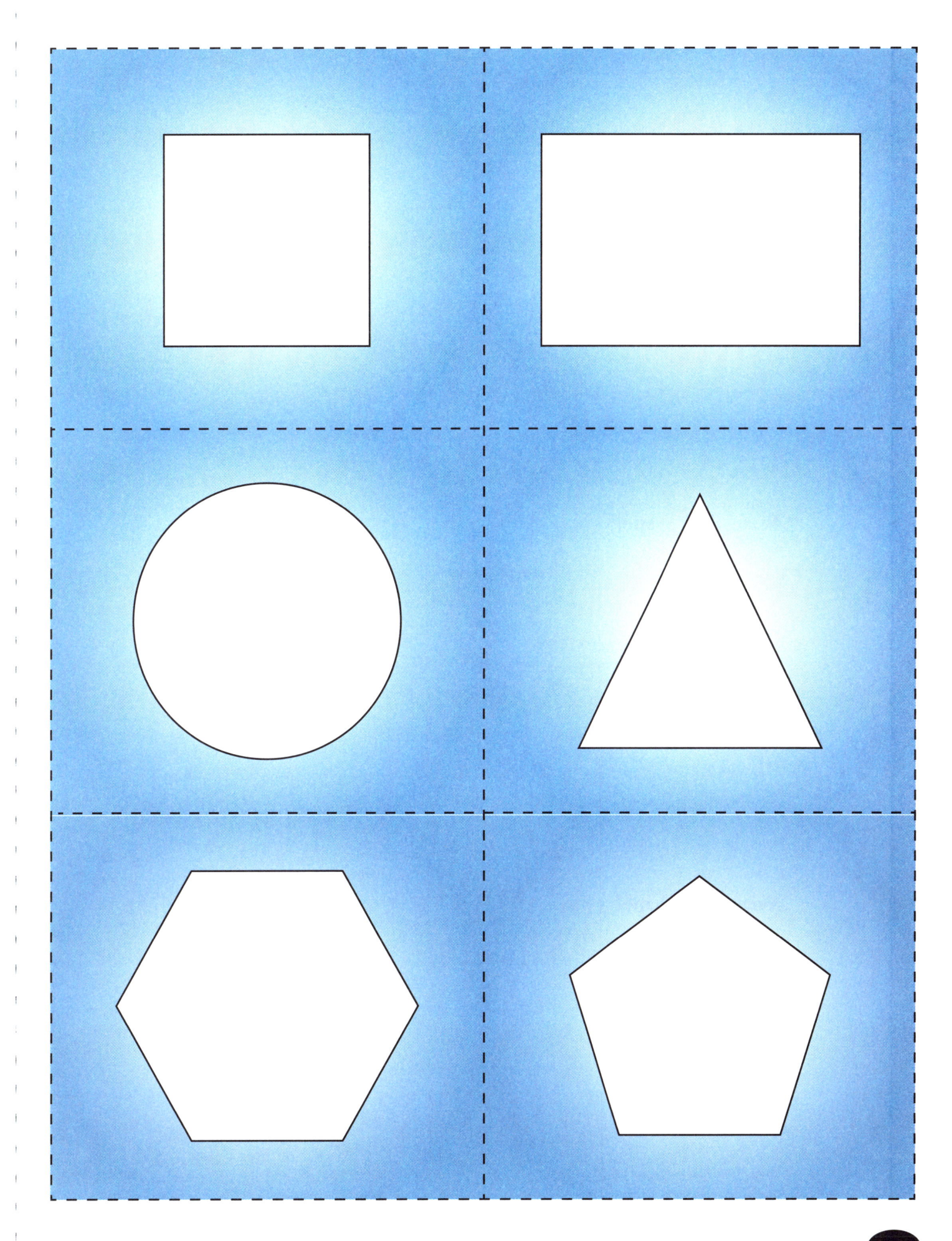

©2004 by Evan-Moor Corp. • Math Centers—Take It to Your Seat • EMC 3021

Name That Shape!
Set 1

EMC 3021
©2004 by Evan-Moor Corp.

Name That Shape!
Set 1

EMC 3021
©2004 by Evan-Moor Corp.

Name That Shape!
Set 1

EMC 3021
©2004 by Evan-Moor Corp.

Name That Shape!
Set 1

EMC 3021
©2004 by Evan-Moor Corp.

Name That Shape!
Set 1

EMC 3021
©2004 by Evan-Moor Corp.

Name That Shape!
Set 1

EMC 3021
©2004 by Evan-Moor Corp.

square	rectangle
circle	triangle
hexagon	pentagon

Name That Shape!
Set 1

EMC 3021
©2004 by Evan-Moor Corp.

Name That Shape!
Set 1

EMC 3021
©2004 by Evan-Moor Corp.

Name That Shape!
Set 1

EMC 3021
©2004 by Evan-Moor Corp.

Name That Shape!
Set 1

EMC 3021
©2004 by Evan-Moor Corp.

Name That Shape!
Set 1

EMC 3021
©2004 by Evan-Moor Corp.

Name That Shape!
Set 1

EMC 3021
©2004 by Evan-Moor Corp.

1
- 4 sides
- 4 square corners
- all sides are the same length

2
- 4 sides
- 4 square corners
- 2 short and 2 long sides

3
- a closed curve
- no corners

4
- 3 sides
- 3 corners

5
- 6 sides
- 6 corners

6
- 5 sides
- 5 corners

Name That Shape!
Set 1

EMC 3021
©2004 by Evan-Moor Corp.

Name That Shape!
Set 1

EMC 3021
©2004 by Evan-Moor Corp.

Name That Shape!
Set 1

EMC 3021
©2004 by Evan-Moor Corp.

Name That Shape!
Set 1

EMC 3021
©2004 by Evan-Moor Corp.

Name That Shape!
Set 1

EMC 3021
©2004 by Evan-Moor Corp.

Name That Shape!
Set 1

EMC 3021
©2004 by Evan-Moor Corp.

©2004 by Evan-Moor Corp. • Math Centers—Take It to Your Seat • EMC 3021

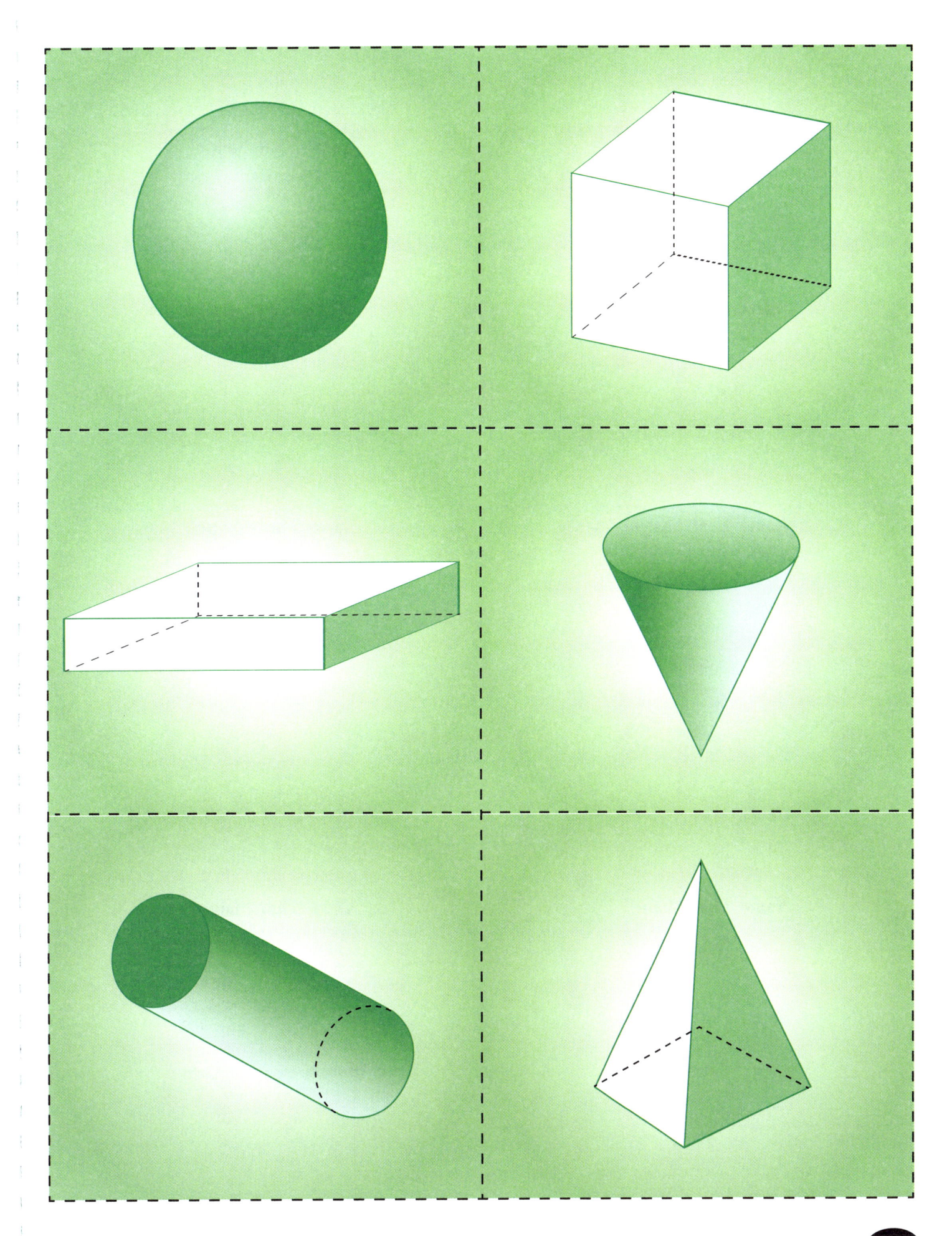

Name That Shape!
Set 2

EMC 3021
©2004 by Evan-Moor Corp.

Name That Shape!
Set 2

EMC 3021
©2004 by Evan-Moor Corp.

Name That Shape!
Set 2

EMC 3021
©2004 by Evan-Moor Corp.

Name That Shape!
Set 2

EMC 3021
©2004 by Evan-Moor Corp.

Name That Shape!
Set 2

EMC 3021
©2004 by Evan-Moor Corp.

Name That Shape!
Set 2

EMC 3021
©2004 by Evan-Moor Corp.

sphere	cube
rectangular prism	cone
cylinder	square pyramid

Name That Shape!
Set 2

EMC 3021
©2004 by Evan-Moor Corp.

Name That Shape!
Set 2

EMC 3021
©2004 by Evan-Moor Corp.

Name That Shape!
Set 2

EMC 3021
©2004 by Evan-Moor Corp.

Name That Shape!
Set 2

EMC 3021
©2004 by Evan-Moor Corp.

Name That Shape!
Set 2

EMC 3021
©2004 by Evan-Moor Corp.

Name That Shape!
Set 2

EMC 3021
©2004 by Evan-Moor Corp.

1
- solid shape
- no faces
- no vertexes
- no edges

2
- 6 faces
- each face is a square
- 8 vertexes
- 12 edges

3
- solid shape
- all 6 faces are rectangles
- 8 vertexes
- 12 edges

4
- solid shape
- 1 face is a circle
- a point at one end

5
- solid shape
- 2 faces are circles
- sides shaped like the outside of a tube

6
- solid shape
- 1 face is a square
- 4 faces are triangles
- 5 vertexes

Name That Shape!
Set 2

EMC 3021
©2004 by Evan-Moor Corp.

Name That Shape!
Set 2

EMC 3021
©2004 by Evan-Moor Corp.

Name That Shape!
Set 2

EMC 3021
©2004 by Evan-Moor Corp.

Name That Shape!
Set 2

EMC 3021
©2004 by Evan-Moor Corp.

Name That Shape!
Set 2

EMC 3021
©2004 by Evan-Moor Corp.

Name That Shape!
Set 2

EMC 3021
©2004 by Evan-Moor Corp.

Place Value Puzzles

Preparing the Center

1. Prepare a folder following the directions on page 3.

    Cover—page 171
    Student Directions—page 173
    Sorting Mats—page 175
    Number Cards—page 177
    Task Cards—pages 179–185

2. Reproduce a supply of the answer form on page 170. Place copies in the left-hand pocket of the folder.

Using the Center

1. The student selects a set of task cards and writes the set number on the answer form.

2. The student takes the envelope of number cards and selects the sorting mat that matches the card set.

3. Next, the student selects a task card and, using the sorting mat and number cards, creates numbers to complete the tasks on the card.

4. Finally, the student writes the numbers he or she used and the resulting answer on the answer form.

©2004 by Evan-Moor Corp. • Math Centers—Take It to Your Seat • EMC 3021

Name _____ Set _____ **Answer Form**

Place Value Puzzles

Write the numbers you used and the answer on the lines.

Card #	Numbers Used	Answer
1		
2		
3		
4		
5		
6		
7		
8		
9		
10		
11		
12		

Bonus:

Set 1: What is the largest number you can make with 4 number cards? _____

Set 2: What is the largest number you can make with 7 number cards? _____

Place Value Puzzles

Math Centers—Take It to Your Seat • EMC 3021 • ©2004 by Evan-Moor Corp.

Place Value Puzzles

Follow these steps:

1. Choose a set of task cards. Write the set number on the answer form.

2. Take the envelope of number cards. Take the sorting mat that is the same color as the task cards you are using.

3. Read a card. Using the sorting mat and number cards, make the number. Write the numbers you used and the answer after the card number on the answer form.

4. Repeat Step 3 until you have completed all of the cards.

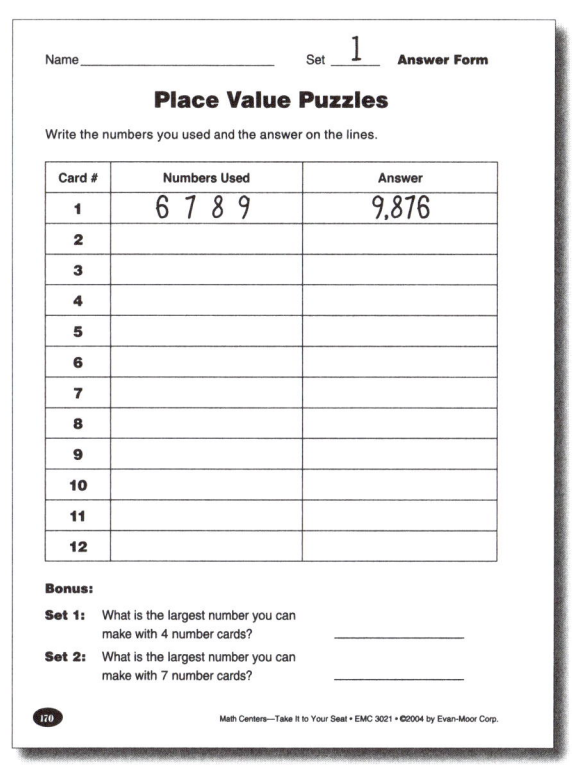

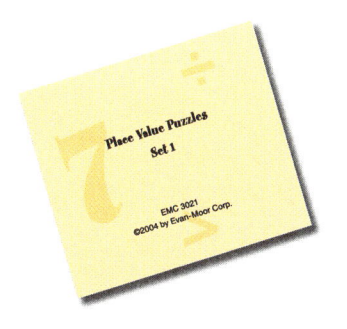

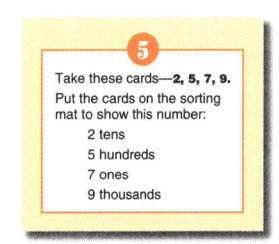

Place Value Puzzles
Sorting Mat
Set 1

[thousands] , [hundreds] [tens] [ones]

Place Value Puzzles
Sorting Mat
Set 2

[millions] , [hundred thousands] [ten thousands] [thousands] , [hundreds] [tens] [ones]

Place Value Puzzles
Set 1

EMC 3021
©2004 by Evan-Moor Corp.

Place Value Puzzles
Set 2

EMC 3021
©2004 by Evan-Moor Corp.

0	1	2	3	4
5	6	7	8	9
0	1	2	3	4
5	6	7	8	9
0	1	2	3	4
5	6	7	8	9
0	1	2	3	4
5	6	7	8	9

178
Math Centers—Take It to Your Seat • EMC 3021 • ©2004 by Evan-Moor Corp.

1

Take 4 different number cards.

Put the cards on the sorting mat.

Make the largest number you can.

2

Take 4 different number cards.

Put the cards on the sorting mat.

Make the smallest number you can.

3

Take 4 number cards. Two of the numbers should be the same.

Put the cards on the sorting mat.

Make the largest number you can.

4

Take 4 number cards. Two of the numbers should be the same.

Put the cards on the sorting mat.

Make the smallest number you can.

5

Take these cards—**2, 5, 7, 9.**

Put the cards on the sorting mat to show this number:

- 2 tens
- 5 hundreds
- 7 ones
- 9 thousands

6

Take these cards—**8, 6, 4, 0.**

Put the cards on the sorting mat to show this number:

- 0 hundreds
- 8 ones
- 4 thousands
- 6 tens

©2004 by Evan-Moor Corp. • Math Centers—Take It to Your Seat • EMC 3021

Place Value Puzzles
Set 1

EMC 3021
©2004 by Evan-Moor Corp.

Place Value Puzzles
Set 1

EMC 3021
©2004 by Evan-Moor Corp.

Place Value Puzzles
Set 1

EMC 3021
©2004 by Evan-Moor Corp.

Place Value Puzzles
Set 1

EMC 3021
©2004 by Evan-Moor Corp.

Place Value Puzzles
Set 1

EMC 3021
©2004 by Evan-Moor Corp.

Place Value Puzzles
Set 1

EMC 3021
©2004 by Evan-Moor Corp.

7

Take these cards—**2, 5, 1, 0.**

Put the cards on the sorting mat to show this number:

    2 tens

    1 one

    0 thousands

    5 hundreds

8

Take these cards—**6, 3, 6, 3.**

Put the cards on the sorting mat.

Make the largest number you can.

9

Take these cards—**4, 0, 0, 2.**

Put the cards on the sorting mat.

Make the smallest number you can.

10

Take these cards—**3, 3, 7, 7.**

Put the cards on the sorting mat to show this number:

    3 tens

    7 ones

    3 thousands

    7 hundreds

11

Take these cards—**5, 6, 7, 8.**

Put the cards on the sorting mat to show this number:

    7 hundreds

    8 tens

    6 ones

    5 thousands

12

Take these cards—**9, 3, 0, 4.**

Put the cards on the sorting mat to show this number:

    9 hundreds

    0 tens

    4 ones

    3 thousands

©2004 by Evan-Moor Corp. • Math Centers—Take It to Your Seat • EMC 3021

**Place Value Puzzles
Set 1**

EMC 3021
©2004 by Evan-Moor Corp.

**Place Value Puzzles
Set 1**

EMC 3021
©2004 by Evan-Moor Corp.

**Place Value Puzzles
Set 1**

EMC 3021
©2004 by Evan-Moor Corp.

**Place Value Puzzles
Set 1**

EMC 3021
©2004 by Evan-Moor Corp.

**Place Value Puzzles
Set 1**

EMC 3021
©2004 by Evan-Moor Corp.

**Place Value Puzzles
Set 1**

EMC 3021
©2004 by Evan-Moor Corp.

1

Take 5 number cards.

Place the cards on the sorting mat.

Make the largest number you can.

2

Take 5 number cards.

Place the cards on the sorting mat.

Make the smallest number you can.

3

Take 6 number cards.

Place the cards on the sorting mat.

Make the largest number you can.

4

Take 6 number cards. Two of the numbers should be the same.

Place the cards on the sorting mat.

Make the smallest number you can.

5

Take 7 number cards.

Place the cards on the sorting mat.

Make the largest number you can.

6

Take 7 number cards.

Place the cards on the sorting mat.

Make the smallest number you can.

©2004 by Evan-Moor Corp. • Math Centers—Take It to Your Seat • EMC 3021

**Place Value Puzzles
Set 2**

EMC 3021
©2004 by Evan-Moor Corp.

**Place Value Puzzles
Set 2**

EMC 3021
©2004 by Evan-Moor Corp.

**Place Value Puzzles
Set 2**

EMC 3021
©2004 by Evan-Moor Corp.

**Place Value Puzzles
Set 2**

EMC 3021
©2004 by Evan-Moor Corp.

**Place Value Puzzles
Set 2**

EMC 3021
©2004 by Evan-Moor Corp.

**Place Value Puzzles
Set 2**

EMC 3021
©2004 by Evan-Moor Corp.

7

Take these cards—**9, 8, 7, 6.**
Put the cards on the sorting mat to show this number:
    8 tens
    7 hundreds
    6 ones
    9 thousands

8

Take these cards—**0, 2, 4, 6, 8.**
Put the cards on the sorting mat to show this number:
    2 tens
    0 hundreds
    6 thousands
    4 ones
    8 ten thousands

9

Take these cards—**9, 8, 7, 6, 5, 4.**
Put the cards on the sorting mat to show this number:
    9 tens
    8 hundreds
    7 ones
    5 thousands
    4 hundred thousands
    6 ten thousands

10

Take these cards—**0, 0, 1, 1, 2, 2, 3.**
Put the cards on the sorting mat to show this number:
    0 tens
    2 hundreds
    1 one
    2 ten thousands
    0 thousands
    1 million
    3 hundred thousands

11

Take these cards—**1, 2, 3, 4, 5, 6, 7.**
Put the cards on the sorting mat to show this number:
    1 ten
    2 hundreds
    6 hundred thousands
    4 thousands
    5 ten thousands
    3 ones
    7 millions

12

Take these cards—**0, 2, 3, 4, 6, 7, 8.**
Put the cards on the sorting mat to show this number:
    3 hundreds
    8 ten thousands
    7 ones
    6 millions
    4 thousands
    0 hundred thousands
    2 tens

©2004 by Evan-Moor Corp. • Math Centers—Take It to Your Seat • EMC 3021

**Place Value Puzzles
Set 2**

EMC 3021
©2004 by Evan-Moor Corp.

**Place Value Puzzles
Set 2**

EMC 3021
©2004 by Evan-Moor Corp.

**Place Value Puzzles
Set 2**

EMC 3021
©2004 by Evan-Moor Corp.

**Place Value Puzzles
Set 2**

EMC 3021
©2004 by Evan-Moor Corp.

**Place Value Puzzles
Set 2**

EMC 3021
©2004 by Evan-Moor Corp.

**Place Value Puzzles
Set 2**

EMC 3021
©2004 by Evan-Moor Corp.

Answer Key

What's Missing?–page 5

Set 1

In-between	After	Before
1. 135	1. 113	1. 854
2. 502	2. 555	2. 257
3. 646	3. 319	3. 162
4. 700	4. 887	4. 184
5. 833	5. 656	5. 300
6. 801	6. 570	6. 489
7. 690	7. 291	7. 930
8. 486	8. 834	8. 721
9. 601	9. 752	9. 679
10. 861	10. 1,000	10. 858
11. 779	11. 378	11. 999
12. 999	12. 861	12. 395

Set 2

In-between	After	Before
1. 2,135	1. 1,313	1. 1,854
2. 5,302	2. 5,155	2. 2,257
3. 8,646	3. 3,019	3. 4,162
4. 7,000	4. 8,987	4. 1,484
5. 3,833	5. 6,456	5. 3,800
6. 1,601	6. 5,570	6. 999
7. 6,900	7. 2,291	7. 5,930
8. 4,854	8. 8,324	8. 8,721
9. 6,010	9. 7,152	9. 6,579
10. 1,861	10. 10,000	10. 6,858
11. 7,579	11. 3,278	11. 9,999
12. 9,999	12. 8,261	12. 3,095

Bonus: Answers will vary depending on the number selected, but must show an accurate sequence of numbers.

Pizza Party–page 15

Set 1

Answers will vary depending on the choices made by the student, but they must correctly reflect the task. For example: $\frac{1}{2} > \frac{1}{4}$.

Set 2:

Answers will vary depending on the choices made by the student, but they must correctly reflect the task. For example: $\frac{5}{6} > \frac{1}{3}$.

Bonus:

Set 1: $\frac{1}{8}, \frac{1}{6}, \frac{1}{5}, \frac{1}{4}, \frac{1}{3}, \frac{1}{2}, \frac{5}{8}, \frac{2}{3}, \frac{3}{4}$

Set 2: $\frac{1}{8}, \frac{1}{4}, \frac{1}{3}, \frac{3}{8}, \frac{1}{2}, \frac{2}{3}, \frac{3}{4}, \frac{5}{6}, 1\frac{1}{2}$

Money Match–page 25

Set 1	Set 2
25¢—Cards 1, 4	$0.80—Cards 2, 4
38¢—Cards 2, 6	$1.25—Cards 1, 5
50¢—Cards 3, 7	$1.93—Cards 3, 8
90¢—Cards 5, 11	$2.00—Cards 7, 12
75¢—Cards 8, 12	$2.55—Cards 9, 11
12¢—Cards 9, 10	$5.00—Cards 6, 10

Bonus: Answers will vary.

The Answer Is...–page 39

Answers may be in a different order, but must be in the correct box.

Set 1

6
15 – 9
10 – 4
12 – 6
3 + 3
5 + 1
4 + 2

7
16 – 9
14 – 7
12 – 5
1 + 6
4 + 3
2 + 5

8
16 – 8
13 – 5
17 – 9
6 + 2
3 + 5
7 + 1

9
14 – 5
17 – 8
18 – 9
4 + 5
7 + 2
3 + 6

Set 2

6
12 – 6
10 – 4
2 × 3
12 ÷ 2
18 ÷ 3
30 ÷ 5

7
3 + 4
7 × 1
16 – 9
14 ÷ 2
35 ÷ 5
21 ÷ 3

8
6 + 2
4 × 2
14 – 6
2 × 4
16 ÷ 2
32 ÷ 4

9
9 × 1
3 × 3
18 ÷ 2
17 – 8
27 ÷ 3
6 + 3

Bonus: Answers will vary, but must be accurate and equal the given answers 6, 7, 8, and 9.

Pattern Puzzles–page 51

Set 1
1. 2, 4, 6, <u>8</u>, <u>10</u>, 12, 14, <u>16</u>
2. 5, 10, <u>15</u>, 20, <u>25</u>, <u>30</u>, 35, <u>40</u>, 45, <u>50</u>
3. 10, 20, 30, <u>40</u>, <u>50</u>, 60, <u>70</u>, <u>80</u>, 90, <u>100</u>
4. 3, 6, 9, <u>12</u>, 15, <u>18</u>, <u>21</u>, 24, 27, <u>30</u>
5. 15, 25, <u>35</u>, 45, <u>55</u>, 65, <u>75</u>, <u>85</u>, 95, 105
6. 2, 22, 3, 33, <u>4</u>, 44, <u>5</u>, 55, <u>6</u>, <u>66</u>

Set 2
1. 9, 18, 27, <u>36</u>, <u>45</u>, <u>54</u>
2. 3, 8, 7, 12, <u>11</u>, 16, <u>15</u>
3. 50, 55, 40, 45, <u>30</u>, <u>35</u>, 20
4. 100, 150, 200, <u>250</u>, <u>300</u>, <u>350</u>, <u>400</u>
5. 1, 3, 2, 4, 3, <u>5</u>, <u>4</u>, <u>6</u>
6. 3, 6, 12, <u>24</u>, <u>48</u>, <u>96</u>

Bonus: Answers will vary.

Exactly the Same–page 61

Set 1	Set 2
1, 12	1, 10
2, 5	2, 14
3, 13	3, 9
4, 9	4, 13
6, 14	5, 16
7, 16	6, 11
8, 11	7, 15
10, 15	8, 12

Bonus: Answers will vary, but must be congruent shapes.

Money Machines–page 75

Set 1

nickel	dime
$0.05	$0.10
$0.10	$0.20
$0.15	$0.30
$0.20	$0.40
$0.25	$0.50
$0.30	$0.60

nickel and penny	one dollar
$0.06	$1.00
$0.12	$2.00
$0.18	$3.00
$0.24	$4.00
$0.30	$5.00
$0.36	$6.00

Set 2

quarter	half dollar
$0.25	$0.50
$0.50	$1.00
$0.75	$1.50
$1.00	$2.00
$1.25	$2.50
$1.50	$3.00

five dollars	one dollar and one nickel
$5.00	$1.05
$10.00	$2.10
$15.00	$3.15
$20.00	$4.20
$25.00	$5.25
$30.00	$6.30

Bonus: Answers will vary.

Perimeter and Area–page 83

Perimeter Set
1. 16
2. 24
3. 28
4. 21
5. 12
6. 12
7. 28
8. 22
9. 18

Area Set
1. 6
2. 9
3. 7
4. 6
5. 5
6. 8
7. 10
8. 7

Bonus for both sets: Answers will vary.

Measuring at the Circus–page 97

Card A
1. about $6\frac{1}{2}$ inches
2. 1 cm
3. 1 cm
4. 1 inch

Card C
1. $6\frac{1}{2}$ inches
2. 2 cm
3. 2 cm
4. 3 inches

Card B
1. 3 cm
2. about 4 inches
3. $4\frac{1}{2}$ inches
4. 3 cm

Card D
1. 15 cm
2. 5 inches
3. $\frac{1}{2}$ inch
4. about 3 inches; about 8 cm

Bonus: Answers will vary.

©2004 by Evan-Moor Corp. • Math Centers—Take It to Your Seat • EMC 3021

Time Flies–page 113

Set 1
1. 12:00
2. 9:30
3. 8:15
4. 3:45
5. 2:00
6. (clock showing 11:30)
7. 3:00
8. 12:00
9. 7:00
10. 3:30
11. 3:00
12. (clock showing 3:30)

Set 2
1. 4:15
2. 8:45
3. 3:20
4. 12:05
5. 7:24
6. (clock showing 9:50)
7. 3:10
8. 6:00
9. 12:45
10. 11:20
11. 2:30
12. (clock showing 3:25)

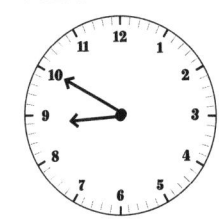

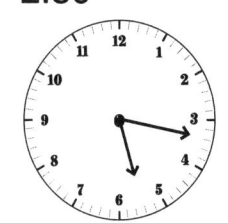

Bonus: Answers will vary, but must contain two clockfaces and a correct calculation of elapsed time.

Read a Graph–page 127

Card 1
1. Carl's fun at camp
2. take a hike, 1 more time
3. paddle a canoe, 4 fewer times
4. bar
5. No. It only tell us that he went swimming more times than anything else.

Card 2
1. picking a piece of pie
2. apple
3. coconut
4. picture
5. No. The graph only shows what kinds of pie people picked.

Card 3
1. a vegetable stand
2. tomatoes
3. squash
4. circle
5. Yes. There is a green squash on the graph.

Card 4
1. favorite sodas
2. 5 kinds
3. Kid Kola
4. circle
5. No. There is no pink lemonade on the graph.

Card 5
1. the number of books George checked out
2. 6 books
3. June
4. picture
5. No. The graph only tells how many books George checked out.

Card 6

1. catching crabs
2. Saturday, 4 more
3. 21 crabs
4. bar
5. No. It does not show Thursday on the graph.

Bonus: Answers will vary, but should relate to the graph and include correct answers.

Make a Graph–page 139

Graphs will vary somewhat, but must show the correct information on the correct graph form.

Set 1

1. 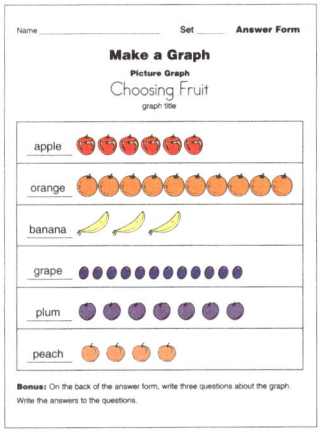
2. 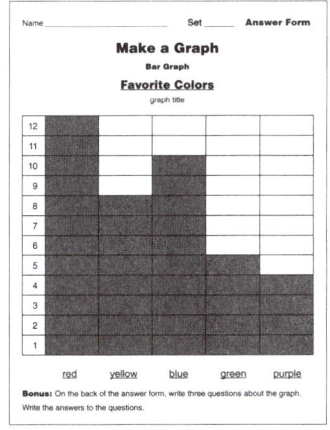
3. 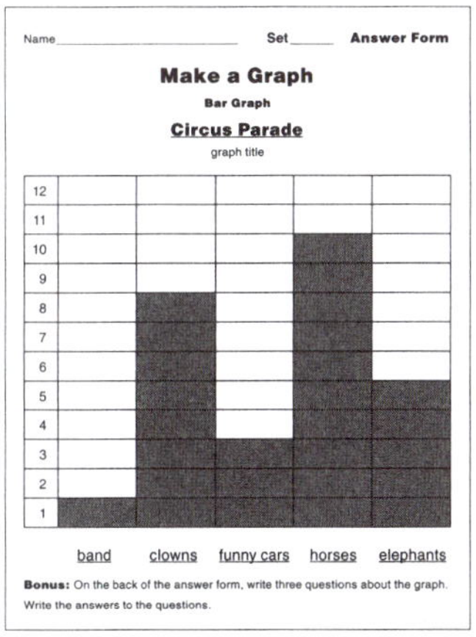
4.

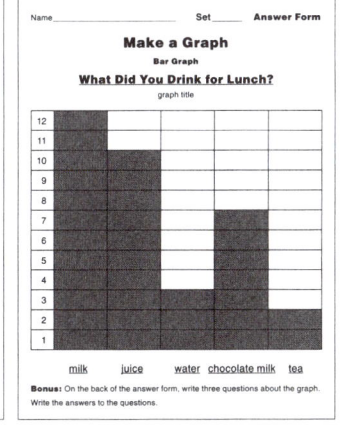

Set 2

1. 
2. 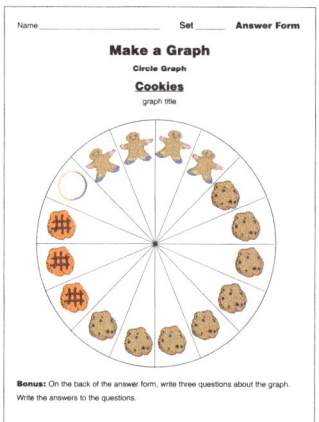
3. 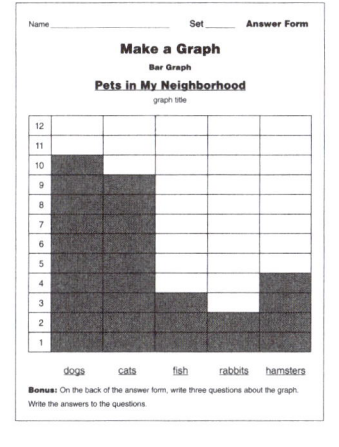
4.

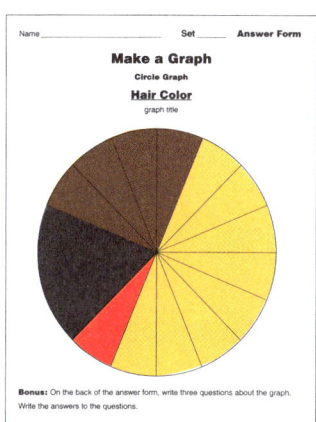

Bonus: Answers will vary, but must reflect information shown on the graph chosen by the student.

Name That Shape!–page 151

Set 1

, square, Card 1

, rectangle, Card 2

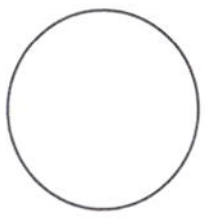

, circle, Card 3

△, triangle, Card 4

⬡, hexagon, Card 5

⬠, pentagon, Card 6

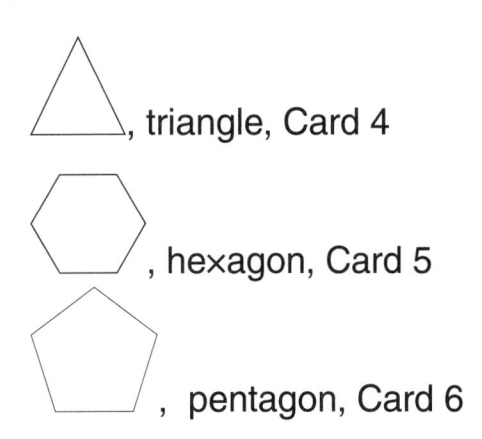

Set 2

sphere, Card 1
cube, Card 2
rectangular prism, Card 3
cone, Card 4
cylinder, Card 5
square pyramid, Card 6

Bonus: Students should draw and name an octagon.

Place Value Puzzles–page 169

Set 1

1–4. Answers will vary depending on the choices made by the student, but they must correctly reflect the task.

5. 9,527
6. 4,068
7. 521
8. 6,633
9. 24
10. 3,737
11. 5,786
12. 3,904

Bonus: Answers will vary, but must be the largest number possible that can be made with the 4 numbers chosen.

Set 2

1–6. Answers will vary depending on the choices made by the student, but they must correctly reflect the task.

7. 9,786
8. 86,024
9. 465,897
10. 1,320,201
11. 7,654,213
12. 6,084,327

Bonus: Answers will vary, but must be the largest number possible that can be made with the 7 numbers chosen.